I0362681

DISCIPLINED FOR LIFE

STEPS TO SPIRITUAL STRENGTH

JOHN LOFTNESS   C.J. MAHANEY

Revised Edition

GENERAL EDITOR: C.J. MAHANEY

EXECUTIVE EDITORS: GREG SOMERVILLE (First Edition)

KEVIN MEATH (Revised Edition)

PURSUIT OF GODLINESS
SERIES
PDI
COMMUNICATIONS

PDI Communications is a division of PDI Ministries,
which serves a growing network of local churches in
the United States and abroad. For information about
the ministry or for permission to reproduce portions
of this book, please contact us.

PDI Communications
7881 Beechcraft Avenue, Suite B
Gaithersburg, MD 20879

1-800-736-2202
fax: 301-948-7833
email: pdi@pdinet.org
Web site: www.pdinet.org

Cover design: Gallison Design
Book design: Carl Mahler

ISBN 1-881039-00-5

Printed in the United States of America

1197

CONTENTS

FOREWORD TO THE REVISED VERSION

This book has its origin in our personal quests to grow closer to God and to find our greatest delight in him. As we have sought to increase in the knowledge of our Lord and the experience of his truth and love, we've become convinced that the spiritual disciplines are an essential means of grace. God stands ready to give, but we must position ourselves to receive.

As with any book or sermon, this material did not develop in a vacuum. We are indebted to many other authors, too numerous to mention here, who have influenced our thinking about the spiritual disciplines. Many of their books are listed in the "Recommended Reading" section at the end of each chapter. Key thoughts are quoted in highlighted boxes throughout the book.

The contents of this revised version are not greatly different from those of the original book. Most of the text changes have been made in Studies One, Two, and Eight, and derive largely from an expanded understanding of the all-pervasive sinfulness of the human heart. While the original book still retains value, and we would not discourage the use of those copies already in circulation, we trust that new readers will be somewhat better served by this revised version. We would, however, encourage small-group leaders wishing to take a group through this book to try to assure that each member is using the same version.

Greg Somerville invested many long hours in the original effort to bring this book to completion. Greg's work reflects more than his skill as an editor; he also leads a small group, and we think you'll appreciate how he has developed questions that encourage group participation and help draw these studies out of the realm of theory and into daily practice.

Assisting Greg in making the original book possible were two gifted and dedicated individuals: production coordinator Beth Kelley and graphic designer Carl Mahler. Their creative suggestions and keen eye for detail helped make each draft better than the last. The revised version benefited significantly from the work of Kevin Meath (editorial) and Martin Stanley (design/production). For the combined expertise and enthusiasm of these two publishing teams we are deeply grateful.

— **John Loftness and C.J. Mahaney**

HOW TO USE THIS BOOK

Disciplined For Life, like each book in PDI's Pursuit of Godliness series, is designed for group as well as individual study. The series is the logical outgrowth of four deeply held convictions:

■ The Bible is our infallible standard for faith, doctrine, and practice. Those who resist its authority will be blown off course by their own feelings and cultural trends.

■ Knowledge without application is lifeless. In order to be transformed, we must apply and practice the truth of God's Word in daily life.

■ Application of these principles is impossible apart from the Holy Spirit. Though we must participate in change, he is the source of our power.

■ The church is God's intended context for change. God never intended for us to live isolated from or independent of other Christians. Through committed participation in the local church, we find instruction, encouragement, correction, and opportunities to press on toward maturity in Christ.

As you work through these pages, we trust that each of these foundational convictions will be reinforced in your own heart.

With the possible exception of the "Group Discussion" questions, the format of this book is equally suited for individuals and small groups. A variety of different elements have been included to make each study as interesting and relevant as possible.

Scripture Text: Begin by going to the source.

Warm-Up: A little mental exercise to get you in the mood.

Personal Study: Here is the meat of the lesson, spiced with occasional questions to help you apply what you're reading.

Margin Questions: If you have the time, dig deeper into the lesson as you *Meditate On...* biblical truths or turn to related passages *For Further Study*.

Group Discussion: Though you may not get past the first question or two, these are guaranteed to get your group thinking and talking about real-life issues.

Recommended Reading: For those who can't get enough of a particular topic, here's a whole bookshelf full of great resources.

While you are encouraged to experiment in your use of this book, group discussion will be better served when members work through the material in advance. And remember that you're not going through this book alone. The Holy Spirit is your tutor. With his help, these studies may well change your life. ■

ONLY ONE THING IS NEEDED

C.J. MAHANEY

SCRIPTURE TEXT Luke 10:38-42

WARM-UP Which makes the most noise?

A. A heavy-metal band
B. A "boom car"
C. A jackhammer
D. A jet
E. A personal CD player
F. A leaky faucet

(See page 9 for answers)

PERSONAL STUDY Had Martha known her temper tantrum would wind up in Luke's Gospel, she probably would have kept a lid on it. But her embarrassment is our gain, for in Luke 10:38-42 we discover one of the most essential (and most neglected) keys to intimacy with God.

The story opens with Jesus and his disciples journeying through the town of Bethany, just two miles east of Jerusalem. It's here, as Luke describes it, that "a woman named Martha opened her home to him."

Now Luke doesn't say, but I'm assuming that Martha opened her home to the disciples as well. Which means she had a minimum of 13 extra place settings to worry about. And it's unlikely that she had an advance schedule of Jesus' itinerary. Every indication is that this was a spontaneous, unexpected visit.

Put yourself in Martha's sandals...Suppose your pastor and twelve of his buddies pulled into the driveway late one afternoon and said, "Jack! Betty! Good to see you! We were just driving by and thought we might stop in and have dinner with you." How would you respond?

1

You would try to look enthusiastic. "What a privilege!" you'd say, a smile frozen on your face. As they came in you would start apologizing for the sink full of dirty dishes, the lawnmower parts spread out on the living room floor. At the same time you'd be mentally rummaging through the cupboards, wondering how you were going to stretch one box of Hamburger Helper into a full-scale banquet.

Can you just see Martha? She's not running a restaurant—she's running a home. If the town of Bethany had a Chinese restaurant or Pizza Hut, she might have tactfully pointed Jesus and his disciples down the street. But that wasn't an option. Martha now has an unexpected crowd for dinner. And though she probably had the best of intentions, it's almost inevitable that some kind of struggle was going on inside her.

> 44 When we fail to wait prayerfully for God's guidance and strength, we are saying, with our actions if not our lips, that we do not need him.[1] 77
>
> — **Charles Hummel**

Being a sincere and industrious woman, Martha buckled down to make a serious meal. It's a fair guess that she assumed her sister Mary—probably her younger sister—would join her in the kitchen. So imagine her reaction when she sees Mary sitting at Jesus' feet, listening to him teach. Here's Martha, sweating over this herculean task of hospitality, while her sister is relaxing, unaware and unaffected. Do you think that may have tested her attitude just a little?

For Further Study:
John's Gospel reveals Martha in a better light. See John 11:17-27 (confession of faith) and John 12:2 (new attitude toward serving).

By this point dinner wasn't the only thing boiling in Martha's kitchen. What began as a genuine act of kindness has taken an unexpected turn. She's now angry, and doing her best to project guilt onto Mary.

"Lord," she snaps, interrupting Jesus' teaching, "don't you care that my sister has left me to do the work by myself? Tell her to help me!"

1 If Mary and Martha's case came to court and you were on the jury, who would you side with? Why?

Martha - she has a "legitimate" claim

Obviously, this was not a polite exchange, and Martha, of course, had no idea it would go on biblical record. But at this point she's a frustrated lady, reacting sinfully to what she felt was real insensitivity.

Martha's reputation has suffered over the years, so let me add this in her defense. She learned from the Lord's tactful and gentle correction, as later accounts in the Gospels make clear. Also, she is to be commended for serving. Serving is a theme emphasized throughout Scripture. It was her sinful attitude, not her serving, that got Martha in trouble.

In seeing activity as a higher priority than listening to the Lord, Martha erred on three fronts.

1. She charged God. "Lord, don't you care...?" To my regret, I have said or thought the same thing many times. If we fail to develop a lifestyle of listening, we inevitably begin to doubt God's love. We become highly susceptible to false interpretations of our circumstances, and are likely to be governed by our emotions.

When we haven't been waiting on God and listening to his voice, we easily become suspicious of his care. Yet few things grieve God more than being accused of not caring. Do you know why? Because there isn't anyone who cares for us like God does. No one cares like the Lord. We will become aware of and secure in his constant care as we study Scripture and listen to his voice.

Meditate on Romans 8:32. Could God have done anything more convincing to reveal his care for us? See also 1 John 4:10.

---

2 Do any of the following circumstances tempt you to say, "Lord, don't you care...?" (Check those that apply)

❑ You're *still* single...with no prospects in sight

❑ You're waiting for the Lord to fulfill a promise he made years ago

❑ You're married but haven't been able to conceive children

❑ You were overlooked for a promotion at work

❑ You've spent the last decade praying and fasting for relatives who still aren't saved

❑ You tithe faithfully but haven't prospered

❑ Other _____

Meditate on Romans 8:28. Don't leave this passage until you are convinced it's true!

2. She became distracted. The American Heritage Dictionary defines "distracted" as "suffering conflicting emotions; distraught." When we don't make time to wait before God, we are easily distracted. Our perspective becomes distorted, our emotions churn, and anxiety begins to build. Martha couldn't have fit that description any better.

And don't think Martha is alone in this—everyone is well-acquainted with distraction and worry. Because when we stop listening, we start worrying, and worry is a serious affront to God. In effect, it says, "I don't trust you, Lord." But when we worship and wait on God, worry is rarely an issue, because in God's presence we receive assurance of his sovereignty, wisdom, and care. Though circumstances may remain unchanged, we now have an eternal perspective which removes the worry from the heart and replaces it with peace.

PSALM 23, ANTITHESIS

The clock is my dictator, I shall not rest.
It makes me lie down only when exhausted.
It leads me to deep depression.
It hounds my soul.
It leads me in circles of frenzy for activity's sake.
Even though I run frantically from task to task, I will never get it all done,
For my "ideal" is with me.
Deadlines and my need for approval, they drive me.
They demand performance from me, beyond the limits of my schedule.
They anoint my head with migraines.
My in-basket overflows.
Surely fatigue and time pressure shall follow me all the days of my life,
And I will dwell in the bonds of frustration forever.

— **Marcia K. Hornok**

---

3 Bible teacher Charles Simpson quotes his father as saying, "Anxiety is a mild case of atheism." What three-word command does Jesus give repeatedly in Matthew 6:25-34?

" _Do_ _not_ _Worry_ "

---

3. She accused and condemned her sister. Failure to wait on God and listen to his voice often culminates in criticism of and comparison to others. We are often tempted to resent others, particularly if they appear "more spiritual." But if we're honest, we'll admit that we sometimes react sinfully to others in exactly the same way Martha reacted to Mary. What this reveals, among other things, is that we haven't been waiting on God.

I'm affected by the way Jesus responded to Martha. He might have stood up and declared, "Do you have any idea who you are talking to? How dare you command me! I created you!" Instead, he sat there, waited until she had

4

finished exposing her sinful heart, and simply said "Martha, Martha."

(By the way…if the Lord uses your name twice, brace yourself for a rebuke. It's time for all seat backs to be placed forward and tray tables to be returned to their original, upright position.)

"You are worried and upset about many things," Jesus told her. "But only one thing is needed. Mary has chosen what is better, and it will not be taken away from her."

> **“** I am the good shepherd; I know my sheep and my sheep know me....My sheep listen to my voice; I know them, and they follow me.[2] **”**
>
> — **Jesus Christ**

Please note that Jesus didn't empathize with Martha. Despite the zeal with which she had served, he didn't excuse her attitude in the slightest. For Martha's activity, although zealous, was neither led by the Spirit nor motivated by God's grace. Rather, it was a work of the flesh, which can snare the Christian in fruitless legalism and dead works. Quite often the result is self-induced frustration, anger, and discouragement.

Once we've been reconciled to God through the person and finished work of Christ, it is important that we cultivate a relationship with God by practicing the spiritual disciplines (worship, prayer, studying Scripture, etc.). In this, let us endeavor to imitate not Martha, but Mary, who in the words of Christ chose "what is better, and it will not be taken away from her." To imitate Mary in her devotion to the Lord is to choose not only the better thing, but the eternal.

For Further Study:
What does it mean to "keep in step with the Spirit" (Galatians 5:25)?

---

4 According to Jesus, what is a distinguishing mark of a believer? (John 10:3-4, 16, 27)

hearing his voice

**Meditate on Matthew
4:4.** What place does
God's Word have in your
daily diet?

A Radically Different Approach

What does it take to please God? To know him more
intimately? To discern his will? To serve his purpose?
First, it takes a listening heart, for discipleship begins
with contemplation, not action.

If you are not regularly hearing God's voice, ask yourself, "Am I regularly making time to listen?" If your schedule reveals that you haven't made listening a priority, you
shouldn't be surprised that you are not having fresh, intimate encounters with God.

Listening requires that we spend unhurried, uninter-
rupted, undistracted time waiting on him. (Jesus instructed
us to find a room where we can go and shut the door
behind us.) Yet many Christians consider prayer a time to
talk *to* God, if not *at* him. But *he* has much to say to *us*,
and we can only hear him if we're listening instead of
talking.

---

5 In which of the following situations would you sense
a need for God's wisdom? (Check all that apply)

☐ Should I finish this chapter or watch some
worthless sitcom?

☐ Should I marry him/her?

☐ Should I practice family planning?

☐ Should I share the gospel with my co-worker?

☐ Should I relocate to accept a higher-paying job?

☐ Should I buy hamburger or tuna fish for dinner?

☐ Should I attend church this Sunday?

☐ Should I go into debt to buy a car?

At the other extreme, we can become overly intense,
trying to *make* God speak. As you wait on him he *will*
speak. He has promised to speak. He is a communicating
God who desires to teach. Remember, we didn't discover
God; he revealed himself to us. There is no divine reluc-
tance to communicate that we must overcome by sheer
force of effort—as if that were in our power.

A primary aspect of listening involves the reading and
study of Scripture. I believe the Holy Spirit desires to

Meditate on John 1:1-2.
Why is it significant that
John describes Jesus as
"The Word"?

apply specific parts of Scripture to the life of each
Christian on a daily basis. This is one of his main ways of
communicating with us. At any given time, each of us—if
we are spiritually healthy—should be able to identify distinct truths from the Bible that the Lord is revealing or
emphasizing to us.

Through Scripture, creation, the church, and by his
Spirit, God fills the world with his voice. The only issue is,
"Are we listening?"

---

6 Give one practical example of how God speaks
through his ...

Creation:

Word:

Spirit:

People:

So let's be provoked by the Lord's example (Mk 1:35),
and not just in the practical aspects such as reading the
Bible in a year or praying 30 minutes a day (as good as
those disciplines are). Let us also be aware that God has
spoken through his written Word and desires to speak by
his Spirit. We have the opportunity to hear our Father's
voice—rich with wisdom, guidance, and affection—if we
will simply devote time to listening and waiting on God.

Intimacy with God can-
not be rushed. Just as every
deep human relationship is
the product of much time,
so it is in our relationship
with God. Jesus maintained
his intimacy with the Father
by meeting with him privately and frequently. Surely if the
Son of God needed this, how much more do we.

> **"** Man is impressed by activity. God is
> impressed with obedience. **"**
> — Terry Virgo

Let's conclude by looking closely at our Lord's
response to Martha. He may be saying the same to you.

1. "Only one thing is needed." What an astonishing statement! How regularly we need to be reminded

that waiting on God and listening to his voice deserve our daily attention. We're talking top priority.

Like our Lord, who had more than a few demands on his life, consciously refuse each day to rush into activity. Instead, devote quality time to expressing your dependence on God and deepening your intimacy with him.

2. Make a choice. Martha may have thought Mary was being lazy and selfish, but listening is far from effortless. It involves discipline and diligence. As Jesus explained to Martha, "Mary has *chosen* what is better" (Lk 10:42). Each day (if not more often), each of us faces a choice. The more we choose as Mary did, the easier the right choice becomes.

3. Recognize what's eternal.

Martha's home cooking was forgotten by breakfast time; Mary's taste of the Bread of Life will last for eternity. She wisely invested in intimacy with God. And as Jesus said, "It will not be taken away from her."

Tomorrow you will make a number of decisions, investing your time and energy in various pursuits. Scripture tells us that one day God will assess our lives. Of the investments you've made today, some will remain, and some may be taken away.

If you follow our culture's advice, you'll invest in a wide portfolio of temporary pleasures. Listening to the voice of the Lord will be low on your priority list. Instead, you will seek to acquire the latest and best material possessions. You will pursue career interests with a blind devotion that neglects family and church. You will indulge in every available form of leisure. And in the process your faith will become that low-cost, convenient, cultural form of Christianity which—tragically—is the norm today.

God's alternative is radical. He is raising up men and women in local churches who are radically different in their passions and pursuits. Radically different in regard

---

THE TYRANNY OF THE URGENT

Prayerful waiting on God is indispensable to effective service. Like the time-out in a football game, it enables us to catch our breath and fix new strategy. As we wait for directions, the Lord frees us from the tyranny of the urgent. He shows us the truth about himself, ourselves, and our tasks. He impresses on our minds the assignments he wants us to undertake. The need itself is not the call; the call must come from the God who knows our limitations. "...The Lord pitieth them that fear him. For he knoweth our frame; he remembereth that we are dust" (Psalm 103:13-14). It is not God who loads us until we bend or crack with an ulcer, nervous breakdown, heart attack, or stroke. These come from our inner compulsions coupled with the pressure of circumstances.[3]

— **Charles Hummel**

to materialism. Radically different in their career goals. Radically different in their use of leisure time. Radically different! Not motivated by legalism, mind you, but in response to his amazing grace. He isn't depriving us of pleasure—he's giving us fullness of joy in his presence! And he is fashioning us into a people who reflect him in order to reach this culture.

As we daily practice the spiritual disciplines, we choose what is better, that which will not be taken away. We will experience the one thing that is truly needed—intimacy with God.

Just like Mary. ■

GROUP DISCUSSION

1. If you were granted a face-to-face meeting with God, and were allowed just one question, what would you ask?

2. When was the last time you found yourself frantically busy? Could you have avoided the rush?

3. Describe one situation where you received a clear word from the Lord.

4. Can you identify with the distorted version of Psalm 23 on page 4?

5. Name two things that make it hard for you to hear God.

6. What should motivate us to be radically different from our culture?

7. How can the spiritual disciplines help us hear God?

RECOMMENDED READING

Spiritual Disciplines for the Christian Life by Donald Whitney (Colorado Springs, CO: NavPress, 1996)

Desiring God by John Piper (Portland, OR: Multnomah Press, 1986)

The Spirit of the Disciplines by Dallas Willard (San Francisco, CA: HarperCollins Publishers, 1991)

TRAIN YOURSELF TO BE GODLY

C.J. MAHANEY

SCRIPTURE TEXT 1 Timothy 4:7-8

WARM-UP Before setting a world record in the 800-meter freestyle at the 1988 Olympics, Janet Evans was swimming 14,000 meters daily. Assuming she only trained for six months (it was probably far longer), we find she logged 183 days x 14,000 meters = 2,562,000 meters. That means she swam 3,203 meters in training for every meter of the final race!

Suppose you spent six months training for a 5-minute witnessing encounter, and that you employed the intensity Janet Evans did when training for the Olympics. How many minutes, hours, and days would your training last?

(See page 22 for answer)

PERSONAL STUDY Developing a relationship with God involves the same dynamics as any skill we might seek to develop. What does it take to master skydiving? The saxophone? Shuffleboard? The same three things it takes to become intimate with God: discipline, practice, and sacrifice.

Now, try to hold your applause. Is that what you expected? Many Christians, whether they would admit it or not, have some vague sense that intimacy with God will miraculously and effortlessly evolve. (Miraculously? In a sense, yes. But effortlessly? Absolutely not.) They believe in the power of the Holy Spirit and grace—as they should—but fail to see the importance of their own effort...

Discipline...

Practice...

Sacrifice.

If we want to develop a closer relationship with God, we've got some work ahead of us.

Practice Precedes Performance

Once when I was a young boy the NCAA college basketball finals were held nearby at the University of Maryland. Because my friend's father had tickets, I was able to go to the game as well as the practice session the day before.

John Wooden, one of the greatest coaches in college basketball history, had again led his UCLA team to the semifinals. The opportunity to get right down on the court and watch this team practice at this level was the closest thing to heaven I had experienced up to that time.

I was a serious sports fan even then, and these UCLA players who came out of the locker room and began their drills were some of my heroes. But the practice session turned out differently than I had expected. There were no slam dunks or behind-the-back passes. Instead, for two hours Coach Wooden rotated his players through numerous drills up and down the court, timing each drill and then moving on to the next. It wasn't exciting. There was no applause, no roar of a capacity crowd. This was all taking place primarily outside of public view.

Their practice was simple and unimpressive—but it's what prepared UCLA to be so effective as they swept their final two games and won the national championship.

Announcers usually overlook details like that. Instead of describing all the sweat and practice that went into a brilliant performance, they tend to focus on the talent and

---

WHEN YOU WISH UPON A STAR

Think of certain young people who idolize an outstanding baseball player. They want nothing so much as to pitch or run or hit as well as their idol. So what do they do?...The star is well known for sliding head first into bases, so the teenagers do too. The star holds his bat above his head, so the teenagers do too. These young people try anything and everything their idol does, hoping to be like him—they buy the type shoes the star wears, the same glove he uses, the same bat.

Will they succeed in performing like the star, though? We all know the answer quite well. We know that they won't succeed if all they do is try to be like him in the game... The star performer himself didn't achieve his excellence by trying to behave in a certain way *only during the game.* Instead, he chose an overall life of preparation of mind and body, pouring all his energies into that total preparation, to provide a foundation in the body's automatic responses and strength for his conscious efforts during the game.

Those exquisite responses we see, the amazing timing and strength such an athlete displays, aren't produced and maintained by the short hours of the game itself. They are available to the athlete for those short and all-important hours because of a daily regime nobody sees.[1]

— Dallas Willard

ability of individual players. Now there's no doubt today's star athletes are gifted. I could spend the rest of my life in training and at no point would I be able to do an effective job of covering Michael Jordan. But if you talked to Jordan or Coach Wooden's UCLA team, they would tell you their public display of astonishing basketball was made possible by the practice which took place in private.

Because such truths so often go ignored and unappreciated in our culture, we can fail to see that skill is of little value without practice and sacrifice. Apart from a private life of sacrifice, discipline, and daily practice—no matter how monotonous—even the most gifted individual will never reach peak performance.

---

1 Which of the following training techniques would be most effective at helping you reach peak potential as a Christian?

☐ Spend the next 40 years in a monastery or convent

☐ Watch three hours of religious programming daily while riding an exercise bike

☒ Devote one entire month to saturating your spirit with teaching tapes, books, and videos + Bible study + Meditation

☐ Imitate the pastor's hair style, hand gestures, and favorite one-liners

☐ Shot-put a durable, 25-pound family Bible in the back yard

☒ Pray and meditate on God's Word for 30 minutes each day

Meditate on 1 Corinthians 9:24-27. For Paul, the prize was well worth the pain. Ask God to fill you with the same passion.

World-class performers are those who count the cost and press on. They don't pity themselves for having to sacrifice time with friends, restrict their diets, or miss the latest cultural attraction. They understand what's required. They understand their need for a demanding daily regimen of practice in order to maintain their edge of excellence and achieve their goal.

If we're serious about deepening our relationship with God and growing in godliness, we will study the private disciplines that helped make Christ effective in public. He is the perfect example. If we can discern and practice those disciplines, we'll see *results*.

13

Working Out in the Wilderness

In the fourth chapter of Matthew's Gospel, beginning in verse one, we find our Lord showing the kind of spiritual strength we'd like to have. Three times Satan tempts him. Three times Jesus turns him away. It's a brilliant performance, a total domination.

Yet our Lord's success was the result of serious preparation: "Then Jesus was led by the Spirit into the desert to be tempted by the devil. After fasting forty days and forty nights, he was hungry" (Mt 4:1-2). These two sentences are very short. It's easy to read them quickly, completely missing the fact that they reveal the source of Jesus' strength. Let's examine them and see what we can learn.

---

2 Check the one spiritual discipline you find most difficult:

☐ Bible study

☐ Private prayer

☐ Group prayer

☐ Worship

☐ Fasting

☒ Solitude/Rest

☐ Other _____

First, Jesus was led by the Holy Spirit. Having learned to wait on the Father for insight and direction, he was very familiar with the Spirit's prompting when it came. That is why, even though the wilderness was not a desirable place to go, when the Spirit directed Jesus there, that's where he went.

He also prepared for his upcoming confrontation by fasting forty days and forty nights. No Big Macs, no Doritos—not even locusts and wild honey. We're talking spiritual discipline. And unlike today's hunger-strikers, he didn't have the national media to cheer him on. He was alone—hungry and alone—for forty days and nights. Discipline. Practice. Sacrifice.

It seems to me Matthew may have been engaging in understatement there in verse 2: "…after which he was hungry." You better believe he was! Not to mention weak. Why would Jesus put himself in such a vulnerable condition

For Further Study:
Some good examples of Jesus' private prayer life can be found in Mt 14:23, Mt 26:36-44, Mk 1:35, Mk 6:46, Lk 5:15-16, Lk 6:12-13, and Lk 9:28.

before this head-to-head confrontation with Satan? Because he knew that while fasting would weaken his body, it would make him strong in spirit.

I think Jesus spent much of those forty days meditating on Scripture. Each time Satan tempted him, he responded with a quote from the book of Deuteronomy. It's my guess that Jesus, reading through his Old-Testament-In-A-Year plan, had wound up in this often-neglected book. Because he was meditating on these passages, he was able to utilize three appropriate verses, wielding them as the sword of the Spirit.

---

3 Find one verse you could use to battle a recurring temptation. Write it in the space below.

For God did not give us a spirit of fear, but of love and of self-discipline and POWER!

Can we understand and appreciate the effort involved here? Do we understand the relationship between Christ's private preparation and his public performance?

Although Jesus overcame Satan's attack in the wilderness through preparation in private, a very different temptation awaited him when he began to minister publicly. Luke records our Lord's response to the pressure of popularity: "Yet the news about him spread all the more, so that crowds of people came to hear him and to be healed of their sicknesses. But Jesus often withdrew to lonely places and prayed" (Lk 5:15-16). It would have been so easy for him to be manipulated by the limitless number of legitimate needs. Instead, he sought his Father in private. It didn't take the disciples long to see that he was intimate with and dependent on his Father; morning by morning he went to a solitary place where he could listen, meditate, and worship. These disciplines weren't an obligation for him—they were his passion. And they were the means by which he received grace to fulfill his ministry and eventually die on the cross.

Meditate on Isaiah 50:4-7. Note how verses 4-5 in this prophetic description of Jesus prepare him for the suffering described in verses 6-7.

These passages are only two examples. Unlike today's sports announcers, the Gospel writers recognized the source of Christ's strength and repeatedly documented his practice of the disciplines. Yet we rarely highlight these verses in our Bibles. They are easily overlooked. We

Meditate on John 5:19-20. If Jesus approached his daily "To Do" list this way, do you think you would benefit from the same kind of guidance?

need to identify and study them as a description of our Lord's daily lifestyle. If we want to emulate Christ's on-the-field performance, we must imitate his off-the-field preparation.

Partners in the Process of Change

Let's now look at two verses which, at face value, seem to give conflicting clues as to the source of our power to live like Christ.

"Now the Lord is the Spirit, and where the Spirit of the Lord is, there is freedom. And we, who with unveiled faces all reflect the Lord's glory, are being transformed into his likeness with ever-increasing glory, which comes from the Lord, who is the Spirit" (2Co 3:17-18). Freedom, as Paul uses it here, implies a freedom from selfishness, freedom from self-gratification, freedom to serve God, freedom to serve others. Also note the word "transformed"—we'll see that stressed again shortly.

This passage emphasizes the necessity of the Holy Spirit in the transforming process. An inner work is needed. It begins with our regeneration—an exclusive work of God—and continues as the Holy Spirit conforms us to the image of Christ.

While only the Spirit can bring about change, God has also given us a vital role in this continuing process of transformation. Paul identifies our responsibility in Romans 12:2: "Do not conform any longer to the pattern of this world, but be transformed by the renewing of your mind. Then you will be able to test and approve what God's will is—his good, pleasing and perfect will."

How are we transformed? By the renewing of our minds. This verse presents a clear command to us. If the Spirit is going to transform us, we must first put ourselves in a position to be transformed by devoting ourselves to the spiritual disciplines, for it is by these that our minds are renewed.

> " Though the power for godly character comes from Christ, the responsibility for developing and displaying that character is ours. This principle seems to be one of the most difficult for us to understand and apply. One day we sense our personal responsibility and seek to live a godly life by the strength of our own willpower. The next day, realizing the futility of trusting in ourselves, we turn it all over to Christ and abdicate our responsibility which is set forth in the Scriptures. We need to learn that the Bible teaches both total responsibility and total dependence in all aspects of the Christian life.[2] "
>
> — **Jerry Bridges**

16

At this point, it would be easy to become confused or misled if we do not keep clearly in mind the distinctions between justification and sanctification, and the role we play in each. Justification occurs—all at once—when we are converted. It is completely and exclusively an act of God. We make no contribution to our justification whatsoever except, as Luther said, our sin which God so graciously forgives. No amount of Bible study, prayer, or fasting can ever become the basis for our justification before God, for we have been declared righteous by God solely on the basis of the person and finished work of Jesus Christ.

For Further Study:
Read Isaiah 64:6 and
1 Peter 1:15-16. In light
of the first passage,
how can we hope to
obey the second?

Once we become Christians, however, the gradual process of sanctification (becoming more like Christ) and the renewing of our minds begins. In this, God is still the central player—the now-indwelling Holy Spirit continually gives us the grace to obey, without which we would live in constant rebellion against God—yet our degree of obedience to God's commands makes a genuine difference, both in this life and for eternity.

So, first we are justified through Christ alone. Then, the *purpose* and *evidence* of our justification is a life of obedience and spiritual growth (sanctification). That's what it means to be a disciple, a disciplined one. Conversion is only the beginning. Our call is to follow Jesus and to reflect his character.

---

4 Check all that apply: *You know you're legalistic when you...*

☒ Stay depressed all day because you slept through your quiet time

☒ Need assurance that you are "doing enough" spiritually to remain in God's favor

☒ Gauge the depth of your spirituality by the length of your quiet time

☒ Look down on other Christians who have never read through the Bible

☒ Feel closer to God because you've gotten up early to pray three days in a row

☒ Attribute God's blessing to your own spiritual diligence

Don't Let Go!

"Have nothing to do with godless myths and old wives' tales; rather, train yourself to be godly" (1Ti 4:7). The last five words of this verse contain three essential insights for us as we explore the spiritual disciplines.

First, note the goal. It's not happiness. It's not success. The goal is godliness. Now that doesn't sell many Christian books, and it certainly doesn't fly on most Christian television, but the Church of Jesus Christ should be characterized by people whose primary motivation is godliness. Rather than making every decision in pursuit of personal prosperity and career advancement, they live for God's glory, placing godliness and servanthood above material gain.

Second, consider the word "train." Paul used the Greek word *gymnadzo* from which we get our word "gymnasium." He chose this term intentionally. The dedicated athlete and the dedicated Christian both submit to intensive training and self-discipline. They spend long hours in private honing their skills, reflexes, and concentration. But where the athlete seeks honor, the Christian seeks intimacy.

> **" Jesus did not possess any special means of spiritual growth which are not available to us. It is essential to realize this if we are to understand Jesus, if we are to become like him.**[3] **"**
>
> **— Sinclair Ferguson**

Third, this verse—like Romans 12:2—places the responsibility for training squarely in our court. Don't ask God to train you. He won't do it. Believe me, I've asked many times. Instead, he'll point you to your spiritual gymnasium with the same advice Paul gave young Timothy: *Train yourself!*

The once-popular, pseudo-spiritual advice to "Let go and let God" may be offered with good intentions, but it's completely unbiblical. A cooperative effort is required. Though God is the one who began and sustains this good work in us (Php 1:6), he commands our participation in the process of sanctification.

Meditate on 1 Peter 1:15-16. Are there any areas of your life where you have concluded that holiness (or godliness) is beyond your reach?

I try to work out at the YMCA three times a week. In the years during which I've kept that schedule, I can't remember ever desiring to go. My body has never communicated, "Hey, let's get there early today! And do a double routine!" Just the opposite. "Don't become a fanatic," it argues. "You worked out two days ago. We need another rest. How about tomorrow? How about if we only go twice this week?" Only because I've determined ahead of time

> **"** The general human failing is to want what is right and important, but at the same time not to commit to the kind of life that will produce the action we know to be right and the condition we want to enjoy.[4] **"**
>
> — **Dallas Willard**

For Further Study:
In Psalm 22, David's emotions swing dramatically. What if he had given up after verse 2?

that the benefits are worth the pain do I end up going.

I'd like to say that my body stops complaining once the decision has been made. But the argument resumes at almost every exercise machine. "Don't do this one today. What if your back gives out? Don't run on the stairmaster as well. All right, if you're going to do it, fine. Just do it at half speed." The only exhilaration I feel at the end of a workout is that it's over and I can go home.

And by the way—whoever comes up with those dumb health-spa commercials has never been to the YMCA where I work out. You won't find a group of joyful, perfectly proportioned people effortlessly lifting weights and enjoying meaningful conversation. Nor is it a fitness fashion show. We're just a bunch of awkwardly dressed individuals working up a sweat.

There's a point to my confession here: this scenario closely parallels my experience with spiritual exercise. Can you relate? I wish something dramatic would take place daily to motivate me for my devotional time…a supernatural wake-up call, perhaps, or an angelic escort down to my study. Yet that hasn't been the case. So I've learned not to evaluate the quality of my devotions by the level of my emotions. Regardless of my enthusiasm before or during my devotional time, the combination of worship, prayer, and Bible study is serving to transform me. No question.

Often our spiritual progress is evident to everyone but ourselves. That is part of the reason God places us in a local church. Where we may have overlooked or underestimated our progress, others can bring encouragement by pointing out the fruit born of our diligent practice of the spiritual disciplines.

One Choice at a Time

By now, the especially zealous reader may be all pumped up at the idea of starting tomorrow with a rigorous spiritual workout. That's great—just make sure your first "exercise" is a careful review of the foundation upon which this new determination is built. Does that foundation consist of a fresh understanding of biblical truth, or merely the temporary energy of emotion? If you hope to persevere in your practice of the spiritual disciplines, you'll need something far more reliable than enthusiasm.

Others of you are reading this with a deepening sense of despair. You say, "You don't know how often I have tried." But I've been in the same place. I am among those countless Christians who at least once have started a new year by saying, "This is it! I will read through the Bible in a year!" By February we're bogged down in Leviticus and falling at least four chapters behind every day. In March, provoked by overwhelming guilt, we try to catch up by reading sixty-eight chapters at a sitting—a truly dynamic experience.

Meditate on Hebrews 3:12-19. What was the consequence of Israel's unbelief?

I understand that such failures can tempt us to discouragement, but I've learned not to submit to it, because discouragement is rooted in pride, self-sufficiency, and unbelief. God's Word says, "I can do everything through him who gives me strength" (Php 4:13). Do you feel hopelessly weak when it comes to the spiritual disciplines? Excellent! You're a perfect candidate for the grace of God, for his promise is explicit: "My grace is sufficient for you, for my power is made perfect in weakness" (2Co 12:9).

---

5 When we share our needs with others, we receive both encouragement and accountability. What specific spiritual goals could you share with a trusted friend?

Did you know you are in training at this very moment? Training takes place one choice at a time. Whenever you sin, you are training yourself in ungodliness. (Unfortunately, most of us have become extremely proficient in that area.) But every time we obey God and resist sin, we train ourselves in godliness. You are training yourself to be godly simply by studying and applying what you find in this book.

If you are frustrated and discouraged with your practice of the spiritual disciplines, here's a word of advice: Don't try to be disciplined for the rest of the year today. Don't try to be disciplined for the rest of your *life* today. Just focus on the next 24 hours.

If you need to cut back on calories, it's not smart to begin by proclaiming, "I will not eat dessert for the rest of my life. Until I die or Jesus returns, I will never, ever eat dessert again!" With that approach, you're setting yourself up for disappointment. Instead, simply focus on skipping dessert today.

Otherwise, your resolve will begin to crumble as soon as the waitress brings the dessert tray around at the restaurant tonight. And once you've made eye contact with that piece of Double Dipped Chocolate Fudge Fantasy, it's all over. "Perhaps I was a bit emotional in my quiet time this morning," you'll think. "I really want to guard against legalism. Isn't there a verse about God 'giving us all things richly to enjoy'? What could be richer than this?" Before you know it, that incredible dessert will be reduced to a few crumbs and a six-ounce bulge beneath your belt.

For Further Study: Read Hebrews 12:1-11. What encouragement do you gain from Jesus' example? Have you resisted sin as violently as verse 4 suggests? What harvest does discipline yield (verse 11)?

So how do you begin to train yourself in obedience in this area? *You don't eat that piece of cake.* Isn't that dramatic? Isn't that profound? The same amazing approach will work for developing the spiritual disciplines. Rather than trying to read through the Bible in a year, begin studying the Gospel of John today. Instead of scheduling 12 hours of prayer for tomorrow, begin the day with 15 minutes. Start small, depend on the Holy Spirit, and practice the spiritual disciplines…one decision at a time.

If you want to grow in intimacy with God, if you want to become more like Jesus, here's the secret: Develop the overall lifestyle we see modeled by our Lord. But don't be deceived. It's going to take time and effort to change your lifestyle and habits. God is aware of that. *We* are the ones who need the patience to persevere.

> 66 One word summarizes the mark of the spiritually mature man or woman —obedience.[5] 99
>
> — Jerry White

And finally, remember that God is eager to give you a fresh discovery of himself. But he doesn't give those discoveries to the casual inquirer. He gives them to the individual who seeks with all his heart. When God finds someone who will pursue him with perseverance, it is his delight to reveal himself. That's the ultimate reward for our grace-motivated discipline. That is the prize we seek as we train ourselves to be godly—an intimate, personal relationship with the God who redeemed us and before whom we'll stand throughout eternity, worshiping in amazement as he reveals himself to us in ever-increasing fullness without end. ■

GROUP DISCUSSION

1. Suppose you're an aspiring author...could you expect to get rich from a first book titled *The Painful Path to Godliness*? What does that say about our culture?

2. Summarize the "secret" of Christ's success. (Pages 14-16)

3. Read Philippians 2:12-13. How can we simultaneously "work out our salvation" *and* let God work in us according to his purpose?

4. What does it mean to be a disciple? (See page 17)

5. Does a lack of emotion indicate that your spiritual disciplines need improvement? Why or why not?

6. The author writes that "No amount of Bible study, prayer, or fasting ever becomes the basis for our justification before God" (Page 17). What then is the purpose of these disciplines?

7. What would it take for you to establish a regular pattern of spiritual exercise?

Answer to Warm-Up
(from page 11): Using Janet Evans' ratio of 3,203:1, your training for a 5-minute witnessing encounter would take 16,015 minutes. That adds up to 267 hours, or a grand total of 11.13 days. With that kind of preparation, you would probably make quite an impact!
  Next question: If Train A leaves Chicago for New York traveling at 37 mph...

RECOMMENDED READING

The Pursuit of Holiness by Jerry Bridges (Colorado Springs, CO: NavPress, 1978)

The Practice of Godliness by Jerry Bridges (Colorado Springs, CO: NavPress, 1983)

Holiness by J.C. Ryle (Hertfordshire, England: Evangelical Press, 1979. Originally published in 1879.)

The Discipline of Grace by Jerry Bridges (Colorado Springs, CO: NavPress, 1994)

PRAYER: DIRECT DIAL TO HEAVEN

JOHN LOFTNESS

SCRIPTURE TEXT Matthew 6:5-16

WARM-UP If you could ask God for one thing today and you knew he would grant your request, what would you ask?

❑ Heal me of my sickness

❑ Restore my marriage

❑ Lead the Indianapolis Colts to a Super Bowl championship

❑ Bring (name)_____ to salvation

❑ Help me find a good job

❑ Blind my mother-in-law to the dust on the piano

❑ Introduce me to my future spouse

❑ Let me win the MegaBucks lottery

PERSONAL STUDY My wife Nancy and I are well known among our friends for the amount of time we spend talking. We don't do it because someone at a marriage seminar told us to. We do it because we love conversation with each other. It's been that way for seventeen years now and began long before we were married. Hardly a day goes by without some time of stimulating, usually intimate, discussion.

As I write this, Nancy has the flu. She's been sick for about ten days now. Five days ago she lost her voice. She can't talk beyond a whisper, and when she does whisper, it causes a painful cough.

Last night we sat on the couch after the children were in bed—a typical time to talk—and both of us ended up frustrated. She whispered, "Tell me what's been on your mind." So I told her. It took three minutes. She wanted to respond with a question or some thoughts of her own, but the coughing wouldn't allow it. We ended up reading the newspaper.

Our love and commitment for each other haven't diminished through Nancy's illness, but we miss the intimacy of conversation. Our relationship with God is the same. We can have a commitment *to* him without an intimate relationship *with* him. But if we want our relationship to grow, we must converse. The Bible calls such conversation with God prayer. Without this conversation our experience with God becomes similar to what Nancy and I have gone through during her bout with the flu: we love each other, but our lack of communication creates a sense of distance.

> **"** When there is little awareness of real need there is little real prayer.[1] **"**
>
> — **Donald Whitney**

Still, we can't take our love for granted and ignore prayer. With the distance of non-communication, love can be tempted to wane. Ask anyone who's been through a marital crisis. So prayer is essential to our life with God.

Prayer is perhaps the simplest yet most profound of the spiritual disciplines. When we pray, we are simply communicating with God. No exotic spiritual hoopla, no mystical rituals—just dialogue. And yet it's a dialogue with the exalted Lord of the universe. We have the amazing privilege of speaking directly to Almighty God! More remarkable still is the fact that he listens, and speaks to us in turn.

To keep us from getting tongue-tied or intimidated, Jesus took great pains to show us how to relate to God. He could have emphasized God's role as Judge or King. Instead, Jesus presented him as Father—the kind of Father who welcomes his children with open arms (Mk 10:13-16). And while some of us may have bad memories of our own dads, our Father in heaven loves nothing better than to sit with us and hear everything that's on our mind.

Meditate on Psalm 34. Does David's fear of God hinder his love for God?

Why Pray?

Prayer changes us as much as it changes the situations for which we pray. This is usually unexpected. There I sit, praying for someone who has a bad attitude toward me, and suddenly I realize that the Spirit is playing his flashlight along the walls of *my* heart. "You seem very concerned about that speck in your friend's eye," he whispers, "but have you noticed the log sticking out of *your* face?" We rarely appreciate this information at first until we realize that God *is* answering our prayer.

Prayer also increases our faith. As I write this, my church is involved in a building program. When I think about the amount of money and effort still needed before our facility is built, I can get discouraged. As I pray, though, and affirm the fact that God is in control of the situation, my perspective changes. Not only do I gain faith that God can pull it off, but I get excited about the part *I* can play in making it happen.

---

1 You've been given the privilege of selecting "History's Greatest Answered Prayer" to be featured in heaven's Hall of Fame. The list has been narrowed down to six contestants. Who would you pick?

❑ Elijah: Called down fire and rain (1 Kings 18)

❑ Moses: Saw God clear a path through the Red Sea (Exodus 14)

❑ David: Killed the giant Goliath with nothing but a sling and a stone (1 Samuel 17)

❑ Jesus: Prayed Lazarus back to life (John 11)

❑ Paul: Was sprung from jail by a supernatural earthquake (Acts 16)

❑ You: When you repent and ask God to forgive you, he does!

Thus far we've not mentioned the most obvious benefit of prayer: It works. When we pray, God unleashes his power. Are you sick? Pray. Need a job? Pray. Want your family to know Jesus? Pray. Facing conflict with someone? Pray. We'll be amazed to see the things our Father does when we ask for his help.

But is this work of prayer really necessary? If God is sovereign and controls the whole world, why do we need to pray? Couldn't God do a far better job without our help?

There are certain things our prayers will never change. For example, Jesus will come back whether we pray or

Meditate on James 5:13-18. What did Elijah, "a man just like us," accomplish through his prayers?

25

not. He will judge the living and the dead. These are fixed events in God's purpose. However, our prayers do have an impact in other areas. There are things God just won't do unless we ask. When we pray for a fellow believer to overcome sin, or for a child to be healed of cancer, our prayers are helping fulfill God's will.

Not that God can't accomplish his purposes without us. As John the Baptist noted, God can raise up stones to do his will if we refuse (Mt 3:9). But our involvement matters to God. He invites us, through our prayer, to help usher in his coming kingdom. Why? I'm not sure we can know beyond the fact that he's chosen for it to be that way. Who am I to question him? The fact of the matter remains that though our efforts be sloppy and often weak, he's chosen to accomplish much of his will through us: an amazing privilege.

> **❝** What the Church needs today is not more machinery or better, not new organizations or more and novel methods, but men whom the Holy Ghost can use—men of prayer, men mighty in prayer.[2] **❞**
>
> **— E.M. Bounds**

The Power of Example

Reading about prayer can be helpful, but watching others pray is even better. I spent 15 months serving a church in Southern California in the late 1980s. Every Tuesday through Saturday the pastoral staff invited anyone who wanted to join them for prayer between 6:00 and 7:00 in the morning. No schedule conflicts there. When the church hit a crisis time, we decided to meet as pastors for an additional hour of prayer on those days *before* the other folks arrived.

I can't say I always came freely. It was part of the job, and my attendance wasn't always exemplary. But God used this imposed discipline in my life. I was praying with men committed to intercession. Not that they did anything fancy. And I could tell they were as tired as I was. Yet their fervency and perseverance made a lasting impact on me. By their example, these men taught me more about praying than any lecture or book ever could. Today I count those prayer sessions among my most precious memories of our time in California.

Jesus' example had an impact on the disciples. The Gospel writer John noted that if everything worth recording about Jesus were put on paper, the world couldn't contain the books they would fill. John had to be selective as did the other Gospel writers. When you consider this, it's remarkable how often Jesus' commitment to prayer gets notice.

Jesus prayed early in the morning (Mk 1:35). I personally find this the best time of day to pray. I've got no appointments. Rarely am I interrupted. The house is quiet. Even the air is still. For those who begin work early in the morning, this may not be practical. But there's no better way to start a day.

Jesus prayed in solitary places (Mk 1:35). From what I've read, the ancients didn't know you could pray silently. The Pharisees felt no inhibition in praying aloud in the marketplace. But Jesus seems always to be looking for a solitary place where he could pray out loud. Do you have a solitary place where you can seek God without distraction? I usually pray in my basement before the children are up (though they love to discover me). When I have more time I like to go to a "lonely" place. In California my lonely place was the Altadena Crest Trail high above Pasadena in the San Gabriel Mountains. Here in Maryland I head for the banks of the Potomac River. Any place where you feel comfortable talking out loud to God will work. (I would caution you, however. Make sure your lonely place is also a safe place.)

> **❝** If I should neglect prayer but a single day, I should lose a great deal of the fire of faith.[3] **❞**
>
> — **Martin Luther**

Jesus prayed after work (Mk 6:45-46). He wasn't driven by a "this is my time to relax" mentality. I'm sure he knew how to kick back and enjoy down-time with his fishing buddies, the disciples, but he also knew that sometimes the end of the day was best spent alone with his Father. At a time when most of us feel we've earned the right to a little leisure, Jesus could be found up on a mountain praying. He knew the difference between relaxing and being refreshed. Those hours spent in communion with his Father renewed him from the pressures of a demanding day.

Jesus prayed in the midst of success and popularity (Lk 5:15-16). The best of times can be the worst of times—at least for our prayer life. Success deceives us into thinking we can get along without God for a while. That's why it's critical for us to acknowledge daily our dependence on him. "Who's responsible for this success, God? You are! Please reduce my head back to its original size."

2 When do you feel the most desperate need to pray?

❑ Before going to the dentist for a root canal

❑ After getting a huge salary increase

❑ During labor and delivery

❑ While being honored for service in the church

❑ When a tire blows out in the middle of rush hour traffic

❑ While driving a new car off the lot

Jesus prayed before making a major decision (Lk 6:12-13). When he chose the twelve apostles, Jesus knew he was choosing the future of the Church. He also knew he was choosing a traitor. He needed God's guidance and grace. During an all-night session of prayer he found both.

If you're facing a major decision—a job change, major purchase, move to another city, or marriage—nothing will clear your mind and straighten your priorities like withdrawing to a lonely place to pray. Before my wife and I were engaged, all our friends seemed to think we were perfect for each other. But I needed to know that God himself was confirming the relationship. So I spent a winter day in a New Jersey state park, sitting by an open fire and praying. By the time I left, I was confident God was giving us the go-ahead. Our marriage has been relatively stress free, but if it is ever severely tested, I know I will find tremendous assurance in remembering that snowy day when God made his will known as I sat and waited and prayed.

Meditate on Psalm 130. Do your prayer times include waiting on God so that he can communicate with you?

A night watch with God can be amazingly fruitful. There's something about the stillness and sense of expectancy we experience in the wee hours that make us very alert to God's voice. So instead of taking a dose of Nyquil next time you find yourself sleepless, consider watching for a while with God.

Jesus prayed with regularity (Lk 22:39). As Luke interviewed Jesus' disciples before writing his Gospel, they must have emphasized the frequency of his prayers. That's why Luke says, "Jesus went out *as usual* to the Mount of Olives," one of his favorite solitary places.

28

Jesus prayed honestly (Lk 22:39-44). As Jesus prayed in the Garden of Gethsemane the night before his crucifixion, he was in anguish. Not only was he going to suffer excruciating pain, but his own Father would reject him as the object of his wrath for the sins of the world—an experience totally alien and horrible to him. If he prayed like some prayers I've prayed under pressure, he could have said: "Well, the big day is almost here, Father. I'm really looking forward to being flogged and nailed to the cross. Thanks for the privilege of serving you in this small way."

> 66 The only alternative to frustration is to be sure that we are doing what God wants. Nothing substitutes for knowing that this day, this hour, in this place we are doing the will of the Father.[4] 99
>
> — **Charles Hummel**

But Jesus was honest, and so Luke records what could seem like a feeble prayer: "Father, if you are willing, take this cup from me; yet not my will, but yours be done." Jesus felt free to express his deepest emotions in a prayer prayed through blood, sweat, and tears. He wanted his Father to understand the intensity of his struggle. But in the same breath he expressed his submission to his Father's will.

It's easy to fall into the trap of telling God what we think he wants to hear even though our fine-sounding words don't agree with reality. It's no use lying to the One who knows everything about us (even things we don't know). Are you honest with God when you pray? Do you go to him and express your deepest desires? Your struggles? Your failings? "Yes, Lord, I snapped at her again. I knew it was wrong, but Lord, I was angry! Did you hear what she said? I'm sorry. Forgive me. Give me power to change."

As we pray honestly, God changes us. And by expressing our emotions in prayer we release them to God, making us far less likely to vent them sinfully in some other context.

When my children were younger, they didn't know how to hide their emotions from me. They were free to laugh and giggle in a way that adults would find embarrassing. They were able to cry deeply without the least concern for what I thought of their tears. That's how we should be with God. He's not impressed with our pious platitudes and our many words. He wants honesty—total honesty. He accepts us even when we're angry, apathetic, or afraid. As long as we're not disrespectful or disobedient, we can express the full range of our emotions without worrying that God will get upset.

For Further Study:
The psalmists were surprisingly honest about their emotions when speaking to God. For examples, see Psalm 22, Psalm 38, and Psalm 88.

Some people have real problems with this. Years of bringing one emotion to God—a kind of bored solemnity that pervades so many church services—seems to inhibit them. To get over this, I recommend reading the Psalms aloud. These are the Church's prayers and they contain honest expression of every emotion known to man: from giddy joy to deep discouragement, from furious anger to intimate affection.

---

3 Which of the following emotions would be hardest for you to share with God?

❑ Doubt ("Do you really care?")

❑ Anger ("Why did you let this happen to me?")

❑ Fear ("Can you really accept me in spite of my sin?")

❑ Grief ("How can I cope with the death of this person I so loved?")

❑ Envy ("When will I own a house like everyone else in the church?")

Praying the Disciples' Prayer

The disciples found their inspiration to pray by watching their Lord pray and then making the connection between his public power and private prayer. But fortunately for us, Jesus left more than his example. He gave his disciples a clear model which has been preserved for us in Matthew 6:9-13. Though commonly called the "Lord's Prayer," I like referring to it as the "Disciples' Prayer," because that's what it was: a method Jesus recommended to his disciples for making their prayers most effective.

Before looking at the prayer itself, remember that Jesus was instructing us *how* to pray, not *what* to pray. This was meant to serve as a pattern, a set of principles—not a mindless ritual. Just before outlining this prayer, Jesus urged his disciples not to pray like the pagans who "keep on babbling for they think they will be heard because of their many words" (Mt 6:7). I find it incredibly ironic that for countless Christians, the disciples' prayer has become exactly what Jesus warned against: meaningless babble. Let's take a careful look at it so we can learn to pray the way Jesus intended.

Meditate on Romans 8:15-16. Express your thanks to God for this amazing and totally undeserved relationship.

"Our Father in heaven"

Jesus starts us off by reminding us that our prayer is based on a special relationship. We're praying to our *Father*. This sets a tone of love and intimacy, not guilt or fear. If we don't begin with this reality in mind, all our other prayers will be skewed with a wrong perspective. The Pharisees thought Jesus was blasphemous for being so presumptuous in designating God as Father. But Jesus wants us to think aright about God. Our God is not "up there" somewhere, distant and aloof. He's near to all who call on him. He's our Father, and he wants to meet our every need.

Yet he is our Father in *heaven*—omnipotent, omniscient, and majestic. He is the King. Our intimacy must be matched by respect.

"Hallowed be your name"

With our relationship firmly established in our minds, we next come to worship. To hallow something means we treat it as holy. Our first motivation in prayer should be God's glory. Before we reel off our list of needs and desires, let's give honor to the Lord and worship him. His interests should come before our interests. Pray that throughout the world his name will be respected, magnified, and treated as holy, precious, and pure. This should be our pre-eminent concern prior to any thought of our own needs.

"Your kingdom come"

God is the Creator, the sovereign Ruler, and the eternal Owner of the universe. Yet the majority of his would-be subjects have followed Satan in rebelling against their true King. Consequently, when we come before God and appeal for his kingdom to come, we are asking that the fact of God's authority be recognized and honored in a particular situation.

This is where I bring most of my requests before God. This is where I regularly cry out for him to change situations that are not yet submitted to him—issues in my own life first, then issues in the lives that I touch, and then issues in larger arenas. "Father, root out my selfish attitude toward time. Help Steve to grasp what the gospel is all about. Bring justice for the unwanted and unborn in our land."

In any place or situation where man's kingdom is exerting influence that is contrary to the purposes of God's kingdom—whether that be one individual's decision or a vote in the United States Senate—we can ask God to come and rule.

"Your will be done"

This petition is really a twin to the preceding one. Here we are asking not that our will be done, but that God's will be done—even if we're not sure precisely what his will may be in a particular instance. It is at this point in prayer that I take the opportunity to bring before God any significant decisions I am presently facing. Once I discern what his will is—through meditation on Scripture and waiting before him—I ask that that desire (which was always God's desire and now, by his grace, is also mine)—become reality.

Our prayers should never be selfish or demanding, but at the same time they should be bold. Although it is obvious that we can never command the Sovereign God to do anything, the twin phrases "thy kingdom come, thy will be done" signify that we are to make the strongest possible entreaty. Thus we see from Scripture that there should be nothing apathetic about our request to see God's kingdom and will fully accomplished.

"On earth as it is in heaven"

Instead of settling for compromise, we should consistently seek God's best. In heaven God's kingdom exists in absolute perfection. Here on earth, as we're all too painfully aware, is another story. Until the day when Jesus comes and establishes a new heaven and a new earth, we pray and work to establish outposts of the coming age. "Lord, as I wrestle with this habit, I don't pray that I could cut down. I pray that I could overcome it and defeat it! Your will be done. Rule in my body and soul just as you rule in heaven."

4 This question has three parts:

■ Write down your biggest practical need (new car, better job, etc.) in the space below. Include today's date.

■ Meditate on Jesus' teaching on prayer found in Mark 11:23-24: "I tell you the truth, if anyone says to this mountain, 'Go, throw yourself into the sea,' and does not doubt in his heart but believes that what he says will happen, it will be done for him. Therefore I tell you, whatever you ask for in prayer, believe that you have received it, and it will be yours." What is pre-eminent here: the mountain, your faith, or God's ability? Which of these three makes the most difference in how we pray?

■ Before continuing with the study, take a minute to submit your need to God. (When the prayer is answered, return to this page and write the details in the margin.)

"Give us this day our daily bread"

The Greek word for "bread" in this phrase is not used anywhere else in the New Testament. For centuries scholars have debated exactly what Jesus was implying.

Augustine, writing in the fourth century, believed this reference to "bread" included three things: physical life, the Lord's supper, and the Word of God. Thus, he saw this as a request for physical needs (clothes, shelter, food), forgiveness of sins, and revelation of God's Word. However, Martin Luther and John Calvin felt Augustine was being overly spiritual. They argued that Jesus was referring only to earthly provision.

Regardless of whose interpretation is most accurate, it's clear that God cares about practical things. He knows we have to pay for housing, for clothes and for food, and he wants us to ask for his help. Here we can come to God with our most basic needs. And here we can meditate on what is truly a need and what is a want that falls outside of God's plans for us for the moment.

It's revealing that Jesus tells us to pray for "this day." Take it as a hint that God expects to communicate with us more than once or twice a week! We need him each day, whether the refrigerator is full or empty.

"Forgive us our debts, as we also have forgiven our debtors"

So often when I come to God, I think first about what I've done wrong and begin by confessing my sins. But that's not how Jesus teaches us to pray. In his prayer we begin with relationship, move to the establishment of his kingdom and will, bring before him our basic needs, and *then* come to search our hearts and confess our sins. As the Spirit searches our hearts, we can confess any sins honestly, humbly, and specifically. I find it helpful to confess my sins out loud—then, rather than thinking about what I've done, I'm making a vocal, conscious acknowledgement. That seems to take more humility, and I need all the humility I can get.

Confessing our own sin softens our hearts to forgive those who have sinned against us. Sometimes renouncing bitterness begins with a commitment but entails a process, too. Once a mortgage loan officer misled me in such a way that we almost lost a house we were to buy. I had a difficult time forgiving him. I certainly couldn't work the offense out with him in a biblical manner since he refused to even consider that he caused a problem. He hardly returned my phone calls. I had daydreams of punching the guy out. But as I repented for my bitterness and kept confessing that I forgave him, I eventually got beyond a commitment to forgive to a genuine experience of forgiveness. Sometimes it will be a battle, but we must prevail.

Jesus adds commentary to this part of the prayer by warning about the grave results of unforgiveness. If we persist in bitterness, we no longer have a problem with

---

A FIRE AND A FORCE

Prayer is no petty duty, put into a corner; no piecemeal performance made out of the fragments of time which have been snatched from business and other engagements of life; but it means that the best of our time, the heart of our time and strength must be given...

The praying which gives color and bent to character is no pleasant, hurried pastime. It must enter as strongly into the heart and life as Christ's "strong crying and tears" did; must draw out the soul into an agony of desire as Paul's did; must be an inwrought fire and force like the "effectual, fervent prayer" of James; must be of that quality which, when put into the golden censer and incensed before God, works mighty spiritual throes and revolutions.[5]

— E.M. Bounds

Meditate on Matthew 18:23-35. What treatment can we expect from God if we refuse to forgive others?

another person; our problem is now with God himself (see vs. 14-15).

"And lead us not into temptation, but deliver us from the evil one"

Our spirits may be willing, but our flesh is weak (Mt 26:41). Each of us knows the temptations that master us. It's wise to focus on them first, particularly if you know that you'll be in situations during the day that provide opportunity for sins common to your flesh.

For Further Study:
Memorize 1 Corinthians 10:13.

One good way to search your heart for unconfessed sin and to pray for protection from future temptation is to inventory the Ten Commandments: pray through issues of idolatry in your life; of using God's name to lie or manipulate; of resting not in Christ's work on the Cross but in your own works; of not honoring parents and other family relationships; of anger, sexual lust, stealing, lying, and desiring things that God has not provided. My list here doesn't quote the commandments directly, but instead represents principles of living I've drawn from them—areas in which I have a tendency to fail and need God's help to overcome.

Sadly, most of the people who pray the disciples' prayer finish in about 18 seconds. Prayed thoroughly, the way Jesus intended, it can take 18 minutes or an hour or more. I've prayed the disciples' prayer this way ever since I was a boy, and except for those times when I lacked faith or concentration I've always been rewarded. Not only does this model give me a sense of direction as to how to pray, but when I'm done praying, I know I'm done. I can walk away from my solitary place of prayer feeling satisfied that I've covered the major points with God in preparation for my day.

Frustrated Still?

Most Christians know that prayer is important. That's why it's so common to feel frustrated or condemned when the topic comes up. We just don't do it. Or when we do, we're left dissatisfied. It's discouraging to wake up at the end of my prayer time with crease marks on my face from where I've fallen asleep on my Bible, or to realize I've spent more time contemplating a fishing trip (yes, I admit it) than contemplating the Lord of the universe.

We can take heart, for we're not alone. Our Father in heaven longs to meet with us. He has sent the Holy Spirit to help us know how to pray and how to increase our motivation. If the following three obstacles remain, recognize them for what they are—lies—and get down to the wonderful business of dialogue with God.

"I don't feel like it." If you wait until you feel like praying, you'll probably never pray. Prayer is work—satisfying work, but it still requires real effort. If your emotional state determines when you pray, consistency will never be a part of your experience.

I used to think people would pray once they mastered certain time management skills, but that theory flopped. Unless prayer is a top priority, people just won't pray. Why isn't it our top priority, then? I think I can answer for all of us: pride. We get the foolish idea that we can get along fine without God. We deceive ourselves by thinking that his loving sovereignty is enough to get us through this life. And it is, if all we want to do is "get through." The Holy Spirit has placed in us the desire to please God, and pleasing him requires knowing his will and doing it. This demands humbling ourselves by worshiping, listening, and petitioning our Lord in prayer.

Meditate on Genesis 32:22-30. Why did God wrestle with Jacob before granting his request for a blessing?

"It's discouraging." Prayer can force us to face sins or problems we'd rather avoid. That can be discouraging. But as saints from the turn-of-the-century holiness movement described it, we're called to "pray through" our problems, to wrestle with them until we have faith that God is in control and will fulfill his purposes.

"I've failed before." The longer we've gone without consistent or effective prayer, the harder it is to start. Rather than moan over the last fifteen months, we should start by simply evaluating the past 24 hours. "Did I pray yesterday? No? Fine—but I'll change starting today." With daily evaluation comes daily motivation which results, without our even realizing it, in a lifestyle of prayer.

Never Give Up

I've never been tried for a crime or involved in a lawsuit, but I've been in enough courtrooms to know that judges can be frightening people. Once you are in their courtroom, they have a power to control your life that you'd rather someone so impersonal not have. They also have a tendency to be cold and cynical. They've seen the worst society has to offer and have often been the subjects of manipulation.

To teach us about how to encounter God in prayer, Jesus told a story of a woman who encountered a judge.

She was a widow and so occupied a position of little power, certainly not enough to get a judge's attention. Her neighbor was harassing her in some way, and since she didn't have a husband to defend her, she turned to the local judge. This may have been a move of desperation because this judge had a reputation: he "neither feared God nor cared about men" (Lk 18:2). In other words, he didn't judge based on absolute standards of justice. Equal justice under law was not the guiding principle of his court. He judged as he pleased, and this insignificant woman didn't please him. So he sent her away without even considering her case.

But this widow was the plucky sort, and knowing that she had to choose between living in an oppressive situation or antagonizing a judge, she kept coming back. Finally, she got the better of the judge. Her persistence wore him out. He ruled in her favor, and reluctant justice was done.

What was Jesus trying to teach here? Not that God is cold, cynical, arrogant, and arbitrary, but just the opposite. If a bad judge responds to persistence, how much more a kind, loving, personal judge who rules on perfect standards of justice? If a widow can get justice before a tyrant, how much more will we get what we need from a loving Father? So don't stop asking. Never give up until you have your answer.

Of course, our prayers don't always seem to work out so neatly. We pray and we pray and end up with what seems to be a partial answer or no answer at all. Jesus promised "justice quickly" in the parable but our results often seem muddled at best. Jesus implies an answer to this paradox by ending the parable with a question: "When the Son of Man comes, will he find faith on the earth?" God wants to build us into a people who don't rely on circumstances but who rely on him for their very lives. If every prayer were answered as soon as we asked, there would be no need to trust.

> 44 Unless in the first waking moment of the day you learn to fling the door wide back and let God in, you will work on a wrong level all day; but swing the door wide open and pray to your Father in secret, and every public thing will be stamped with the presence of God.[6] 77
>
> — Oswald Chambers

We began this chapter by noting that prayer is the means of communication in our relationship with God. When prayers are yet to be answered, we either give up or we trust. When we trust, our relationship grows, and in the multi-faceted wisdom of God, we change, other people and circumstances change, and finally our prayer gets answered. But best of all, we grow in love with a mysterious God whose ways we cannot fathom, yet who daily invites us to come to him as Father. ■

GROUP DISCUSSION 1. Why is it that we're nervous about being honest with God?

2. Does God rely on our prayers to accomplish his will?

3. Where is your solitary place for prayer?

4. What's the difference between relaxation and refreshment? (See page 27)

5. Our dependence on God can be measured by the consistency of our prayer. Assuming total dependency measures 6 feet, how "tall" is your prayer life?

6. Are you motivated or intimidated by Jesus' example in prayer?

7. Do you understand the Disciples' Prayer well enough to try using it as a model for your own prayer?

8. What common obstacles keep you from praying effectively?

RECOMMENDED READING *Teach Us to Pray,* D.A. Carson, ed. (Grand Rapids, MI: Baker Book House, 1990)

Desiring God: Meditations of a Christian Hedonist by John Piper (Sisters, OR: Multnomah Books, 1996)

George Mueller: Delighted in God! by Roger Steer (Wheaton, IL: Harold Shaw Publishers, 1981)

MEDITATION: NOT JUST FOR GURUS

JOHN LOFTNESS

SCRIPTURE TEXT Romans 12:1-2

WARM-UP The Barna Research Group has conducted an extensive survey of America's "biblical literacy." Complete the following to see how you compare with the national average:

A. During any given week, how often do you read the Bible?

☐ Daily   ☐ One day a week

☐ Several times a week   ☐ Never

B. Who preached the Sermon on the Mount?

C. Is the Book of Thomas in the Bible?

D. How many apostles did Jesus have?

E. Where does the Bible say, "God helps those who help themselves"?

(See page 52 for survey results)

PERSONAL STUDY All couples fight. Styles of conflict may differ, but friction is inevitable. This is true for any two people who relate closely, be they roommates, co-workers, siblings, or lab partners. But because marriage is such an intimate relationship, fights between spouses are some of the most intense.

Nancy and I found this out soon after we married. She was used to cold warfare, I to Churchillian debates on the floor of Parliament. When conflict arose she withdrew behind a Berlin Wall of silence while I launched into emotional debate. She became intimidated. I got frustrated. The conflicts got worse.

So we talked about it, just the two of us, and we looked into the Bible to get some wisdom. We began to realize that our styles of handling conflict reflected worldly patterns of living that needed to change. We asked ourselves these questions: What does it mean for a husband to love his wife in the midst of a fight? What does it mean for a wife to submit to her husband when she'd rather catch the first plane out of town? What does it mean to "not let the sun go down on your anger"? How is it that "a soft answer turns away wrath"? We prayed together about these issues and asked God to help us apply the Bible's principles. We also asked him to help us resolve conflicts more quickly and learn something productive from each one.

In effect, what we did was practice the spiritual discipline of meditating on God's Word with the purpose of changing our thinking...and our lives.

"Stop allowing yourself to be molded by means of the spirit of this world, but continue to be transformed in your soul by renewing your mind," Paul told the Romans.[1] In our marital conflicts, my mind had been molded to fight in a selfish, aggressive way that hurt Nancy and damaged our relationship. How did this happen? The "spirit of this world" used past examples and experiences to get me to believe this was the way to fight. My mind had adopted manipulative methods rather than the Bible's clear command to be "gentle, not quarrelsome" (1Ti 3:3). Though I was certainly out of line, my behavior was not unique. Often our thinking conforms to the world's pattern and we're not even aware of it.

> **"** Why does the intake of God's Word often leave us so cold, and why don't we have more success in our spiritual life? Puritan pastor Thomas Watson has the answer. 'The reason we come away so cold from reading the Word is, because we do not warm ourselves at the fire of meditation.'[2] **"**
>
> — **Donald Whitney**

When the Spirit shed light on my failure to communicate lovingly with Nancy, I then became responsible for reprogramming my thoughts. That's the partnership Paul describes in Romans 12: God reveals, but we must renew. Insight and power for change come from the Holy Spirit, but the initiative must come from us. For me, that meant imitating a different mode of behavior when I disagreed with Nancy. It required making a conscious effort to speak softly to her. I had to make understanding a higher priority than self-expression. Sometimes I fail and revisit my old pressuring ways. But thanks to her patience and my practice, this is no longer a problem in our marriage.

1 What was the first lifestyle change you made after becoming a Christian?

Meditate on Philippians 4:8-9.
What one excellent or praiseworthy thing can you meditate on today?

What areas of your life have been shaped by the world's mold instead of God's mold? Is there some habit of your flesh that sin has deeply ingrained in your soul? Do you struggle with an enslaving habit, self-pity, uncontrolled anger?

Your Father in heaven knows your symptoms. He also knows the cure: renewing your mind through meditation. Each day, as the Spirit reveals through Scripture where change is required, you can mentally discard wrong patterns of thinking and mentally acquire righteous patterns. Not only will you be shutting out the darkness, but you will be turning on the light: "And we, who with unveiled faces all reflect the Lord's glory, are being transformed into his likeness with ever-increasing glory, which comes from the Lord, who is the Spirit" (2Co 3:18).

A Bad First Impression

What do you think when you hear the word "meditation"? Many imagine someone with a name like Maharishi sitting cross-legged on the ground, eyes closed, chanting a meaningless word over and over until he experiences cosmic revelation. It's no wonder we're a little hesitant when it comes to practicing biblical meditation.

Eastern religions and Christianity approach meditation very differently. In his book *Song of Ascents*, E. Stanley Jones quotes a famous swami in India who taught his disciples, "Kill the mind and then, and then only, can you meditate." It's different for Christians. Instead of emptying our minds, we seek to fill them with God's truth. Instead of listening to nothing, we're listening to God to see what he wants to say. Biblical meditation involves

For Further Study:
Read 1 Kings 19:11-13.
What sign alerted Elijah
to God's presence? Do
you find that significant?

looking at the Word, comparing it to our lives and to the world we live in, and then responding with concrete changes.

Meditation might seem more attractive if the Holy Spirit communicated at the urgent, breathless pace of a radio broadcaster or if the Scriptures read like the cover of a news magazine. That's not the case, however. The Word and the Spirit speak an earth-shaking truth, but quietly. Sometimes we have to strain our ears to hear. Sometimes the Spirit withholds the meaning of Scripture to get at something else in our lives. The problem is not in his speaking but in our listening. He will not force us to listen to him. He comes and quietly says, "I've got something I'd like to say to you. I'll just wait patiently until you are quiet enough to listen."

> **" Let us represent him unto our minds as we find him described in the Gospel; and there we shall behold the perfections of the Divine nature, though covered with the veil of human infirmities; and when we have framed unto ourselves the clearest notion that we can of a being, infinite in power, in wisdom, and goodness, the author and fountain of all perfection, let us fix the eyes of our soul upon it, that our eyes may affect our heart; and, while we are musing, the fire will burn.**[3] **"**
>
> **— Henry Scougal**

Although this chapter will cover a number of practical techniques for meditating effectively on Scripture, it's the end result—hearing and obeying God—that really matters. Imitating someone else's method can be helpful in getting started, but what is important is that whatever we do we stick to eliminating distractions, filling our minds with truth, and then waiting.

Distractions

Overcoming a fear of meditation is only the first obstacle in our path. We still face three adversaries, as missionary and martyr Jim Elliot wrote, that can easily rob us of delight during these intimate times with God. "I think the devil has made it his business to monopolize in three elements: noise, hurry, crowds....Satan is quite aware of the power of silence."[4]

Noise. Back when I was in high school I used to think I could do my homework in front of the TV. For some reason Archie Bunker was always more interesting than trigonometry! It doesn't take much volume for the TV or radio to distract us from the discipline of meditation.

Most of us have noisy minds. I can be in a perfectly quiet place trying to meditate and my mind suddenly kicks into high gear and drives me down some country lane that leads to nowhere. We might as well admit there are a lot of things initially more interesting than Scripture. Regardless of what distracts us, though—pressures, responsibilities, or a lack of discipline—we need to learn to quiet our minds.

Hurry. Modern technology has greatly accelerated the pace of most everyone's life. Microwave ovens, fax machines, and computers have made every second more significant. I sometimes find myself living in overdrive. Two days into vacation, when I've finally slowed down enough to relax, Nancy will jokingly remark, "Good to see you've finally arrived!" The Lord probably feels much the same. It's extremely difficult to meditate when we're always in a hurry. To meditate we must first slow our bodies, then our minds so we can focus on the matters at hand. This is why I find the early morning my best time for meditation; my mind has yet to get wound up with the "to do's" of the day.

> **"** Are we training ourselves only in Christian activity, as good as that may be, or are we training ourselves first of all in godliness?[5] **"**
>
> — **Jerry Bridges**

---

2 Do you show any of the following signs of a hurried lifestyle?

- ❏ You are often a few minutes late to work or meetings
- ❏ You get to the store and realize you've forgotten your purse
- ❏ Back home, you realize you've forgotten the groceries
- ❏ You put your cup full of coffee in your briefcase
- ❏ You frequently have indigestion
- ❏ Your checkbook balances once every third leap year

Crowds. Some of us are always around people. Fellowship and outreach are great, but depending too much on interaction with others is unhealthy. There's a certain security and affirmation we can only get from our relationship with God, and that relationship requires time alone with him. The silence might be intimidating at first. In time, though, these moments away from the crowd—these private encounters with God—will become a source of great strength and joy.

How to Open Your Ears

The first priority, as we've already mentioned, is finding a quiet time and place where you will be as free from distraction as possible. Ruthlessly carve this out of your schedule. If Jesus could duck miracle-hungry crowds to spend time with his Father in solitary places, surely we can escape the demands of prime time television or home repairs.

The next step after choosing a time and place is to prepare your heart. As with all of the disciplines, a variety of methods will do—use whatever works best for you. I like to begin by reading the Word. If I'm groggy, I read aloud. Usually I like to pray through the Disciples' Prayer after I've listened to the Word since Scripture tends to add content to my prayers. Sometimes I don't have the concentration for this so I begin with worship and thanksgiving. These disciplines prepare me to meditate on God's Word with a right perspective.

Meditate on Psalm 95:2 and 100:4. How does thanksgiving prepare us to come before God?

Once your heart is ready, it's time to engage your mind. We should approach Scripture with the fundamental assumption that God speaks uniquely through his Word. The Bible attests to itself as being a living book. Consequently, we don't merely stuff our minds with the facts and principles of Scripture. That would be lifeless. Instead, we listen to what God is saying as to how to apply his Word.

This does not mean we should neglect background studies in the Scriptures. The Bible is an ancient book written over the course of more than 1,400 years by a variety of writers from a variety of cultures. To handle it accurately, we must seek a rudimentary grasp of what the writers meant in their own life context. The scope of this book cannot include Bible study methods, but there are lots of excellent materials available on the American market (some are listed at the end of this chapter), and chances are your church offers classroom Bible instruction. Some of my most life-changing insights have come during often tedious background studies of Bible personalities and books.

As true as it is that God speaks through his Word, we have to train ourselves to hear and recognize his voice. That's powerfully demonstrated in the following story by Bruce Olson, a missionary to the jungles of Colombia. We can learn as much as he did from this hunting expedition with the Motilone Indians:

"Our intrusion into the jungles had brought the usual reaction from assorted birds and monkeys that day, but as we quietly slipped through the dense undergrowth, I noticed a sudden escalation in the volume and intensity of the cacophony. Millions of katydids joined the animal squawks and screeches, raising the noise level to the point where our human voices were nearly drowned out. I'd never heard anything like it. Astonished, I'd turned to a nearby Motilone and shouted, 'Listen to that! Isn't it incredible?'

> **" God is here and He is speaking—** these truths are back of all other Bible truths; without them there could be no revelation at all. God did not write a book and send it by messenger to be read at a distance by unaided minds. He spoke a Book and lives in his spoken words, constantly speaking his words and causing the power of them to persist across the years.[6] **"**
>
> **— A.W. Tozer**

"The Indian had nodded his agreement. 'Yes,' he'd called back, 'we heard it too. It's a piping turkey!' His remark had stopped me in my tracks. A piping turkey? All I'd heard was chaotic, ear-shattering racket! How could anyone notice the voice of one lone turkey in the midst of this din?

For Further Study:
Read Matthew 11:15. What does Jesus mean by this? What's the difference between hearing and listening?

"The Motilone had signaled me to stop and listen quietly. When I did, it took several minutes before I began to pick out which sounds were which—animals, birds, insects, humans. Then slowly, the separate voices became more and more distinct. Finally, after more patient listening, I heard it. Behind the hue and cry of the jungle, behind the voices of my companions, behind the quiet sound of my own breathing, was the haunting, reedy voice of the piping turkey, sounding for all the world like it was calling to us from inside a hollow tube.

"It had been a poignant moment for me, a moment that had spoken to me of much more than the Motilones' highly developed sense of hearing and my own lack of auditory discriminations. It had made me wonder what I'd missed—not only in the jungles, but in my own spiritual life. How much had I overlooked when I'd failed to patiently 'tune in' to God's subtle voice in the midst of life's clamor and activity?"[7]

45

3 What "squawks and screeches" make it difficult for you to listen to God's voice?

❑ The latest *Sports Illustrated*

❑ A sink full of dirty dishes

❑ The sound of my own snoring

❑ Pressures at home or work

❑ Money problems

❑ School assignments

❑ Sports interests or hobbies

❑ An infinite loop of questions from my permanently curious two-year-old

---

Meditate on Joshua 1:8. Would a superficial, 5-minutes-a-day Bible study plan have given Joshua the strength and wisdom he needed to take the Promised Land?

When studying the Bible, how can we sift through all the other noises—cars, trains, lawnmowers, the television, furnace, children—that compete for our attention? If, like Olson, we concentrate on listening, we will slowly learn to recognize the Spirit's voice applying the Scriptures to our life situation. With time it will become easier and easier to distinguish his voice from all the rest. Toward that end, here are some introductory steps to meaningful, meditative Bible study.

Pick your passage. Hit-and-miss Bible study saps motivation. It's far better to have a plan, even if you don't consistently meet it. There are several different kinds of plans you can use:

■ Book studies (Acts, Proverbs, James, etc.)
Goal: Thoroughly study the themes and context of one portion of Scripture.

■ Doctrinal studies (holiness, grace, justification)
Goal: Discover what the Bible as a whole says about one subject.

■ Bible people (Joseph, David, Peter)
Goal: Learn how ordinary people followed God. This can be very encouraging, especially if you study the life of someone with traits or circumstances similar to your own.

■ Character themes (anger, pride, talking too much)
Goal: Obtain God's perspective on a character issue as well as his guidelines for character growth.

■ Bible promises (peace, joy, provision)

Goal: Receive specific assurance for difficulties you face. For example, if you've lost your job, look up everything the Bible says about God's provision.

As you are choosing your course of study, ask the Spirit to guide you to passages relevant to your current situation. Systematic study is important, but God also wants us to study according to our life situation. Are you having trouble with your parents? Study the biblical relationships between parents and children. Are you considering a major purchase? Study the Bible's principles on finances. Are you facing a lot of pressure? Look up what the Bible says about peace and anxiety.

> **❝** I think a new world will arise out of the religious mists when we approach our Bible with the idea that it is not only a book which was once spoken, but a book which is now speaking.[8] **❞**
>
> **— A.W. Tozer**

I like to work from a plan but remain open to change when a topic stimulates my thinking. For example, recently I decided to study Paul's epistle to the Philippians, for no other reason than that I felt it was time to look at one of Paul's letters. I read some introductory material from a few commentaries and used a study booklet by Donald Baker from the InterVarsity Press (IVP) series to guide me in my meditation. If a particular passage intrigued me I would look it up in the commentaries to see what others had said about it.

For several weeks I plugged along without any astounding insights, though I was usually refreshed just from doing the study. But then I hit the fourth chapter of Philippians and read of Paul's contentment regardless of his material prosperity. I felt challenged by this, so when I finished my Philippians study I moved to Randy Alcorn's life-changing book *Money, Possessions, and Eternity* (Tyndale House, 1989). I also started reading through the book of Proverbs, copying down every passage that refers to the use of money. As a result of my study and meditation, I currently find my attitudes toward debt and savings in the middle of a major reorientation. Every morning for the past week I've been profoundly affected by the Scriptures and their application to my family's use of money. Nancy and I are looking at our budget and making changes as a result of meditating on the Word. In the future, during times of meditation that aren't so rich, I will remind myself of the life-changing experience that emerged from a line-upon-line study of the book of Philippians.

What's the most challenging decision or situation you currently face?

Which of the Bible study plans above would serve you best in responding to the challenge you just described?

Take small bites. Your mother's advice is as true for Bible study as it is for eating: small bites of God's Word are easier to digest. Reading Romans in one sitting gives you an overall sense of the book's purpose, but it doesn't lend itself to meditation. It's much better to read only a few verses and get something out of them than to plow through several chapters without any sense of relevance or application. For meditative Bible study, focus on one or two short passages of Scripture so you have plenty of time to digest all that's there.

> ❝ We fail in our duty to study God's Word not so much because it is difficult to understand, not so much because it is dull and boring, but because it is work. Our problem is not a lack of intelligence or a lack of passion. Our problem is that we are lazy.[9] ❞
>
> — R.C. Sproul

Explore the text. There's usually far more to a passage of Scripture than meets the eye. The excitement of Bible study comes as the Spirit reveals hidden treasure in verses we may have skimmed over hundreds of times.

Several strategies serve this purpose. Start by reading the passage aloud and repeating it over and over. Instead of rushing on to the next verse, linger over anything that catches your attention. If you have time, memorize a verse. Then begin asking questions, probing the text from every possible angle. "Lord, how do you want me to renew my mind through this passage? What did James mean when he wrote this about considering it joy when we face trials? What kinds of trials was he facing? What trials am I

For Further Study:
Read Acts 17:11. What distinguished the believers in Berea? Could the same be said for you?

facing? How can I overcome my tendency to complain and rejoice instead?"

In the book *Martin Luther's Quiet Time*, Walter Trobisch includes four simple questions that Luther used to enrich his own personal devotions. With each passage he read during his times of meditation, Martin Luther asked himself:

What am I grateful for?

What do I regret, or what makes me sad?

For what can I intercede?

What am I to do?

Put it in your own words. If you understand what you're reading, you should be able to paraphrase it in your own terms. This simple strategy makes it much easier to remember what you've learned. If you can't put it in your own words, give the passage a little more study.

Get personal and specific. When you read Paul's first letter to the Corinthians, it's unlikely that his thoughts on meat sacrificed to idols strikes you as relevant. I have yet to see a display in my local supermarket that says, "Temple Meat! 50% Off!" Before going on to the next passage or closing your Bible, though, try to make some personal application. If meat sacrificed to idols no longer tempts Christians to compromise, what does? Secular music? Miniskirts? Recreational shopping? A few beers? Cable TV? What tempts *you* to compromise, and what are you going to do about it?

---

5 Which of the following, in your opinion, would require the most urgent and careful study?

❑ Professional licensing exam (nursing, law, etc.)

❑ First skydiving jump

❑ Piano recital for 1500 people

❑ Harvard lecture on nuclear physics

❑ Talk show appearance as an "expert" on abortion

❑ The quest for godliness

The Bible is our sole norm of faith and practice. It is our final authority. Bruce Milne writes in his book *Know The Truth*, "If we are to know who God is, who we are,

Unless we hold tightly to the principles of Scripture, we'll be "blown here and there by every wind of teaching" (Eph 4:14). See Paul's urgent appeal for sound doctrine in 1Ti 4:16, 2Ti 4:3-4, and Tit 1:9.

Meditate on Psalm 1.
How does the picture in verse 3 show the benefits of meditation?

and what God wants of us, we need to study Scripture." The suggestions I've presented may be enough to get you started, but I would strongly suggest that you investigate the books recommended at the end of this chapter. They are full of practical ways to make your Bible study more productive and enjoyable.

Keeping a Journal

Keeping a journal is an excellent way to record and preserve what God shows you. To use a phrase coined by John Wimber, it documents your "private history" with the Lord. Nancy has journals describing her interaction with God that go back to her teenage years. What a treasure! The simple act of writing out our thoughts focuses our meditation and makes us less prone to distraction.

Here are some other specific ways in which a journal contributes to our meditation:

It enables us to track God's curriculum for us. We know by faith that God has a plan and purpose for our lives. But when we look through pages from the preceding months and years, we can see just how God has been unfolding that plan.

It nurtures us during dry times. Our growth in Christ seems to be seasonal. Sometimes we recognize his voice daily; at other times our meditations seem desert-dry. When our feelings no longer provide motivation to seek God, a journal reminds us of the things he has already said and done in our lives. This gives us grace to persevere until the fruit returns.

6 When God led the Israelites through the Jordan River into Canaan, he told them to erect memorial stones as a sign of his faithfulness (Jos 3-4). Put up one "stone" in the space below by describing a specific act of God's faithfulness to you.

It gives us hope for the mundane. Incremental change is almost unnoticeable. Day to day, our journal entries probably won't appear too impressive. But when we look back and see how God's daily building blocks have added up, we'll be surprised at what has actually taken place in us.

It builds our faith for personal change. When our first three children were all aged four and under, Nancy felt her motivation for ministry in the church eclipsed her motivation for motherhood. She was dissatisfied with this and often struggled to reconcile what she viewed as two competing missions in her life. At that time she wrote in her journal, "Lord, make me a woman who has passion for her children!" She prayed this prayer regularly and supplemented it by reading godly books on parenting.

God answered her prayer. She now sees there is no conflict. Motherhood is as much ministry as anything else she does. She still serves our church with passion, but has become equally passionate about training our children. She has the two in such balance that she now can do both guilt free. Without those early journal entries to remind her, she might not realize how much she has changed.

> ❝ The whole Bible has this aim and this power: to create hope in the hearts of God's people. And when hope abounds, the heart is filled with joy.[10] ❞
>
> — **John Piper**

There are a few guidelines you should consider when starting a journal. Above all else, keep it simple. Don't attempt to maintain a comprehensive diary with pages and pages of notes. A few sentences will do. Also, be creative with your journal entries. Write down quotes, dreams, Bible passages, excerpts from books you're reading—anything to inject life into your time. Be completely honest with God as you express what's on your heart. Finally, make sure *God* is your focus. Avoid becoming too preoccupied with yourself or with your style of writing. These notes aren't intended for public consumption so you need not become self-conscious.

Meditate on Matthew 7:24. What's more important than hearing God's words?

Meditating on God's Word teaches us to think biblically. If we take seriously what the Holy Spirit writes on the tablets of our hearts (2Co 3:3), we will sustain the power of his instruction by putting it down on paper. Better yet, we'll go one big step further by obeying what he says. When he gives us treasures through our meditation on his Word, let's learn from the parable of the talents and put his gifts to work (Mt 25:14-30). It's a great way of ensuring that the treasures keep on coming. ∎

1. A.W. Tozer writes, "The Bible will never be a living book to us until we are convinced that God is articulate in his universe." What do you think he means?

2. Can you think of one area where the Holy Spirit has helped you renew your mind? What areas still need work?

Answers to Warm-Up
(from page 39): (A) 12% of Americans say they read the Bible daily; 15% read it several days each week; 16% read it one day each week; 58% don't read it at all. (B) 58% did not know that Jesus preached the Sermon on the Mount. (C) 48% didn't know the Book of Thomas is *not* in the Bible. (D) Only 29% knew Jesus had 12 apostles. (E) The Bible *doesn't* say, "God helps those who help themselves." Seven out of ten Americans missed that.

As Barna's report concluded, "It is the rare American who not only acknowledges that the Bible is the fundamental resource to be used in shaping a philosophy of life, but who also follows through on that belief."[10]

3. Why do we first need to change our thinking before we can change our behavior?

4. How would you describe the difference between Eastern meditation and biblical meditation? (See pages 41-42)

5. Once we discard wrong patterns of thinking, how can we make sure they don't return?

6. Did Bruce Olson's jungle experience seem relevant to your efforts to hear God? Why or why not?

7. Rate your current experience with Bible study: Very exciting, Somewhat exciting, Middle of the road, Somewhat lifeless, Very lifeless.

8. Describe any experience you've had with keeping a devotional journal.

9. How much can we expect to hear from God if we don't obey what he says?

10. If the FBI investigated our claim that we are submitted to the Bible's authority, what evidence would they find in our lifestyle?

RECOMMENDED READING

Knowing Scripture by R.C. Sproul (Downer's Grove, IL: InterVarsity Press, 1977)

The Joy of Discovery in Bible Study by Oletta Wald (Minneapolis, MN: Augsburg Publishing House, 1975)

Tabletalk magazine, published by Ligonier Ministries in Lake Mary, Florida contains a month's worth of daily Bible reading with commentary

Words of Life by Leland Ryken (Grand Rapids, MI: Baker Book House, 1987)

Words of Delight by Leland Ryken (Grand Rapids, MI: Baker Book House, 1992)

FASTING: WHEN HUNGER = POWER

JOHN LOFTNESS

SCRIPTURE TEXT Colossians 3:1-12

WARM-UP How much grain does the average American citizen eat per year in comparison with people living in other nations?

■ USSR	1685.8 pounds
■ European community	976.5 pounds
■ Japan	687.7 pounds
■ China	661.7 pounds
■ Less developed countries	321.2 pounds
■ United States	????.? pounds

(See page 64 for answer)

PERSONAL STUDY Fasting, biblically defined, is abstaining from food for spiritual benefit. For most people, fasting ranks right up there with walking barefoot on hot coals, chanting mantras into the night, or taking a bath in goat's milk. As a child I recall telling my mother that I was "starving" when dinner was an hour late. But skipping dinner altogether? When you don't even have the flu!?

Many people in our consumptive society lack the insight that sometimes it is better to deny yourself a good thing in order to attain something even better. That's the case with fasting: by denying ourselves food, we experience a few hunger pangs and a bit of physical weakness in order to grow in intimacy with God and explore new vistas of his truth and grace.

The Purpose of Fasting

Fasting is a biblical practice, not a biblical command. If you have not fasted until now in your Christian life, don't live in fear that you have been disobeying God. You haven't.

For most Jews of Jesus' day, fasting was a common practice, rooted not only in their Bible and commentaries but in their culture as well. The Pharisees fasted twice a week—on Wednesdays and Fridays. In the Sermon on the Mount, Jesus' phrase "when you fast" (not "*if* you fast") shows he assumed this was a regular activity. And though other religious groups criticized him and his disciples for not fasting enough, Jesus predicted that when he—the bridegroom— left the scene, his disciples would fast (Mt 9:15). This last example seems to imply that those of us following Jesus today will participate in the spiritual discipline of fasting.

> **❝** Behind many of our besetting sins and personal failures, behind the many ills that affect our church fellowships and clog the channels of Christian service...lies that insidious pride of the human heart.... Fasting...is a divine corrective to the pride of the human heart. It is a discipline of the body with a tendency to humble the soul.[1] **❞**
>
> — **Arthur Wallis**

1 Is your view of fasting...

❏ Negative   ❏ Positive   ❏ Non-existent

Briefly describe your thoughts in the space below.

Jesus felt no obligation to match the self-righteous intensity of the Pharisees when it came to fasting. He saw that their motive was to impress others—perhaps even

Meditate on Matthew 6:16-18. How can your face betray your motive during fasting? What rewards do we get from men when fasting? From God?

God—with their display of spirituality. People usually respect such outward signs of commitment, but God looks deeper. "Was it really for *me* that you fasted?" he asked the pious Jews of the period following the Babylonian captivity (Zec 7:5). The physical practice of fasting won't make us more spiritual, but it can open doors that we've yet to enter in terms of knowing God and delighting in his presence. As we look now at the host of reasons why we *should* develop this biblical habit, let's strike self-righteousness from the list.

Fasting yields insight and understanding from God. Are you confused about something in life? Do you need direction? Are you puzzled by a difficult part of Scripture? Fasting can position you to receive God's answers to your questions.

Daniel was a man of tremendous influence in Babylon and King Nebuchadnezzar's wisest counselor. Yet when the prophet read Jeremiah's prophecy that the Israelites would be in captivity for 70 years (Jer 29:10), he was stumped. So in the ninth chapter of Daniel we find him fasting and asking God for understanding. While in the midst of his prayer, Daniel receives God's hand-delivered message from the angel Gabriel. "As soon as you began to pray," said Gabriel, "an answer was given, which I have come to tell you" (Da 9:23).

We can't expect Gabriel to show up each time we skip lunch, but we can fast with a biblical expectation that God will give us the insight we need.

Fasting helps us master the desires of our flesh. There's a snack room at my office where I can buy candy bars for only a quarter. Recently I found I had slipped into the habit of visiting the snack room every afternoon at around 2:00 for a little boost to my taste buds and my belly. I wasn't hungry; lunch was only one hour past. I'd simply taught my body to enjoy that kick of fat and sugar every mid-afternoon. And though my waistline didn't show the effects, I felt God put his finger on my sweet tooth. So I stopped my afternoon candy breaks. For a while I really missed them, my mind sending that "You're starving!" message because my body wasn't getting its food fix.

> ❝ The constant propaganda fed us today convinces us that if we do not have three large meals each day, with several snacks in between, we are on the verge of starvation. This, coupled with the popular belief that it is a positive virtue to satisfy every human appetite, has made fasting seem obsolete.[2] ❞
>
> **— Richard Foster**

Candy bars are a minor obsession compared to something like cigarettes, alcohol, or inappropriate sexual excitement. But if through fasting you can learn to subdue your craving for food, you can gain control over lots of other areas as well.

Paul was determined that nothing other than the gospel of Jesus Christ would master him (1Co 6:12). He disciplined his body so that it would be his slave (1Co 9:27). As fellow servants of Christ, we need to develop the same attitude. If God reveals that we have an undisciplined craving for anything—coffee, nicotine, Diet Coke, or candy bars—we need to show our flesh who is in charge. Fasting is an excellent place to start. This counts for any area of life that needs discipline: control over what goes into our mouths can lead to control over what comes out in the form of anger, gossip, or boasting.

---

2 What's one regular activity that you would really miss if it were removed from your schedule? (Examples: Reading the newspaper, drinking coffee, eating dessert, paying your income tax, etc.)

Would you be willing to lay it aside for a month to make sure it hasn't mastered you?

❑ Yes ❑ No ❑ Not sure

Meditate on 2 Corinthians 12:9-10. How does our weakness make room for God's power?

Fasting humbles our souls. Just before the Israelites crossed the Jordan into the Promised Land, Moses reminded them of what they had learned in the wilderness: "Remember how the Lord your God led you all the way in the desert these forty years, to humble you and to test you...He humbled you, causing you to hunger and then feeding you with manna, which neither you nor your fathers had known, to teach you that man does not live on bread alone but on every word that comes from the mouth of the Lord" (Dt 8:2,3). But the Israelites quickly forgot. Once they entered Canaan, a land "flowing with milk and honey," they strayed from their dependence on God.

When life is comfortable and we have everything we want—good food, a nice place to live, financial security—

it's easy to forget the One who has given us such blessings. We're prone to say, as Moses warned the Israelites, *"My power and the strength of my hands have produced this wealth for me"* (Dt 8:17). Fasting is a great way to clear our minds of that delusion. Fasting takes away our sense of independence and lets us experience our powerlessness before the Lord.

In Psalm 35, David says, "[I] humbled myself with fasting" (v.13). When I fast, I feel weak. It sometimes feels like I've chosen a day of self-imposed sickness. I've never begun a period of fasting thinking, "Oh, this is great! No food for a whole day!" Sometimes I get headaches, and on fasts of more than a day I can get dizzy if I stand up too fast. Twenty four hours of fasting makes me weak and tired. But it's a weakness that I highly value because it reminds me of my absolute dependence on God and his mercy. It is this heightened sense of dependence that I consider to be the most valuable result of fasting.

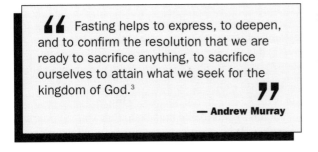

❝ Fasting helps to express, to deepen, and to confirm the resolution that we are ready to sacrifice anything, to sacrifice ourselves to attain what we seek for the kingdom of God.[3] **❞**

— **Andrew Murray**

3 Chances are you don't have to look far to find evidence of pride or independence in your own life. Write down one recent example in the space below.

Fasting prepares us for challenging tasks. At different points in biblical history we find people fasting in anticipation of a significant challenge. Ezra was one of the leaders who brought the Jews back from Babylon to rebuild Jerusalem. Before setting out on the long, dangerous journey he called a corporate fast to ask God's protection (Eze 8:21-23). Jesus launched his public ministry with a

40-day fast (Mt 4:1-3). This time also equipped him to face the incredibly attractive propositions of Satan. Paul and Barnabas received confirmation of their sense of call to apostolic ministry during a time of worship and fasting (Ac 13:2-3).

Are you facing a significant or difficult decision? Is there a crisis in your life? Do you need grace for the week of vacation you'll be spending with non-Christian relatives? Whether the challenge is spiritual or secular, consider preparing yourself with a fast.

Fasting sensitizes us to poverty and injustice. The Jews in Isaiah's day exhibited all the outward signs of righteousness. But God revealed through the prophet that their fasting and religious zeal was hypocritical. Why? Because it didn't affect their hearts. "On the day of your fasting, you do as you please and exploit all your workers. Your fasting ends in quarreling and strife, and in striking each other with wicked fists" (Is 58:3,4).

Throughout Isaiah 58, God calls for a fast that goes beyond ceremony. "Is not this the kind of fasting I have chosen: to loose the chains of injustice and untie the cords of the yoke, to set the oppressed free and break every yoke?" (v.6) A fast should make us more aware of God *and* more aware of those around us. If we keep our eyes and hearts open, God will reveal human needs whereby the spiritual discipline of fasting can spill over into physical benefits as well.

Meditate on 1 John 4:20-21. Do you see how God values our horizontal relationships with others as much as our vertical relationship with him?

---

4 What is one opportunity you have to address injustice or oppression in your community?

Fasting aids us in intercession. The prophet Jeremiah recorded this promise from God: "Then you will call upon me and come and pray to me, and I will listen to you. You will seek me and find me when you seek me *with all your heart*" (Jer 29:12-13, emphasis added). Fasting is an expression of wholehearted zeal, as we find in the book of Joel: "'Even now,' declares the Lord, 'return to me with all your heart, with fasting and weeping and mourning'" (Joel 2:12). This may be a reason why we don't sense God's help or direction in our trials. He's looking for fervent searching—a searching that is greatly aided by fasting.

Fasting adds muscle to our spiritual warfare. When Jesus sought spiritual power to withstand the devil and accomplish God's purpose, he fasted. The Bible describes countless individuals and even entire nations who gave up their food to change the course of history by fervent intercession.

> **44** Fasting is designed to make prayer mount up as on eagles' wings. It is intended to usher the suppliant into the audience chamber of the King and to extend to him the golden sceptre. It may be expected to drive back the oppressing powers of darkness and loosen their hold on the prayer objective. It is calculated to give an edge to a man's intercessions and power to his petitions. Heaven is ready to bend its ear to listen when someone prays with fasting.[4] **77**
>
> — **Arthur Wallis**

Some Practical Guidelines

Types of fasts. Scripture indicates several different ways to fast:

The normal fast. When I first experimented with fasting, I thought I had to give up everything. I was into the second day when my aunt asked, "Are you drinking any water?" "No," I answered, "I'm fasting." She proceeded to set me straight and spare me from dehydration.

A normal fast excludes food but includes water. At the end of Jesus' 40-day fast, Scripture says he was *hungry* (Mt 4:2). Had he not drunk water during that time, apart from supernatural intervention not indicated in the text, his body wouldn't have made it. In Scripture, absolute fasts are a rare exception. Both Esther and Paul went three days without food or water (Est 4:16, Ac 9:9), but their situations were desperate. An absolute fast should be clearly directed by God and should never exceed three days.

The partial fast. After a particularly disturbing vision, Daniel spent three weeks on a "luxury free" diet. As he describes it, "I ate no choice food; no meat or wine touched my lips; and I used no lotions at all until the three weeks were over" (Da 10:3). If your work schedule is so demanding that you can't cope without food, consider

For Further Study:
Fasting is so effective that it can cause God to reverse his judgment (see Jonah 3, 1 Kings 21:17-29). Arthur Wallis writes, "Because man repents in respect to sin, God repents in respect to judgment. Strictly speaking, then, it is not God that really changes, but man."[5]

something along the lines of Daniel's model. A juice fast, for example, is completely acceptable, though you should avoid anything high in refined sugar as well as citrus juices (unless they are fresh).

God doesn't evaluate our fasting by the length or totality of our abstinence from food. He cares only for its effect on our hearts. If a partial fast works well with your schedule and accomplishes God's purpose, don't let anyone tell you it's insufficient.

The corporate fast. It's a little-known fact that Abraham Lincoln designated April 30, 1863 as "a day of national humiliation, fasting and prayer." He did this at two other times during his presidency; before him, Presidents John Adams and James Madison had done the same. In each case the nation sought God's help as it faced the prospect of war.

Corporate fasting results in multiplied power. Jesus said, "For where two or three come together in my name, there am I with them" (Mt 18:20). Churches and nations can expect an outpouring of God's power and grace when they band together in properly motivated fasting and prayer. Throughout the Old and New Testaments we see God's people feasting and fasting corporately, as noted above in the case of Paul and Barnabas in Acts 13.

Planning ahead. The main value of fasting lies not in its ability to impress God, but in the way it sensitizes us to him. Our hunger has no inherent benefit unless it brings us to our knees before God. So don't fast just for the sake of fasting. Enter your fast with a strategy for how you will spend the time and what you hope to accomplish. This will reinforce your motivation and sharpen your concentration. Also, don't make the mistake of gorging yourself

---

A PRESIDENTIAL PROCLAMATION

"We have been recipients of the choicest bounties of Heaven. We have been preserved, these many years, in peace and prosperity. We have grown in numbers, wealth, and power as no other nation has ever grown. But we have forgotten God. We have forgotten the gracious hand which preserved us in peace, and multiplied and enriched and strengthened us; and we have vainly imagined, in the deceitfulness of our hearts, that all these blessings were produced by some superior wisdom and virtue of our own. Intoxicated with unbroken success, we have become too self-sufficient to feel the necessity of redeeming and preserving grace, too proud to pray to the God that made us! It behooves us, then, to humble ourselves before the offended Power, to confess our national sins, and to pray for clemency and forgiveness."

— From the text of a proclamation made by President Abraham Lincoln on March 30, 1863 calling for a national day of humiliation, prayer, and fasting.

For Further Study:
As you have time, look at some of the occasions where Israel responded to a national crisis by fasting (Jdg 20:26ff; 1Sa 7:5-13; 1Sa 31:11-13; 2Ch 20:1-30).

before a fast—it just makes withdrawal from food all the more difficult. It's best to make your last meal a light one, especially if you intend to fast longer than 24 hours.

If you have a medical condition like diabetes, check with your doctor before fasting. The same would apply for pregnant or nursing women.

The importance of prayer. Even if you can't set aside time for concentrated prayer, fasting has value as a means of dedication and consecration to the Lord. However, I benefit most from fasting when I take time to make prayer a priority. At the very least, take the time you'd normally spend eating to feast on communication with your Father. Let's take advantage of this time when our spiritual senses can be sharpest.

Working your way up. If you have never fasted, don't think you need to begin with 40 days alone in the desert. A horrible first experience will make it hard for you to consider fasting again. Instead, consider the following progression:

24-hour juice fast. Begin in the evening (after dinner) by consecrating the time to God in prayer. During the following day, drink juice and pray in lieu of breakfast and lunch. Conclude by eating dinner.

24-hour water fast. Same as the above, but drink water instead of juice. You'll find yourself weaker, but you should be able to miss two meals without any significant effect on your work.

36-hour water fast. By skipping your evening meal you can add 12 hours to your time of fasting. It doesn't matter whether dinner is the first meal or the last meal you miss. The schedule isn't important. Experiment to find what makes your times of fasting most fruitful.

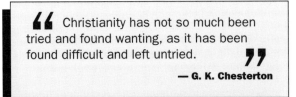

66 Christianity has not so much been tried and found wanting, as it has been found difficult and left untried. **99**

— G. K. Chesterton

Three-day water fast. I try to schedule this type of extended fast at a time in my calendar when God can do a complete spiritual check-up. Some may do this routinely; others may consider a three-day fast as intimidating as running a marathon. If you're in that second category, this story may encourage you.

Years ago I had a friend who, after hearing that I was going on a three-day retreat to fast and pray, gave me a look of horror. His religious background made him suspect I was doing this out of some legalistic obligation. He found it nearly impossible to understand why anyone would choose to subject himself to such extended torture voluntarily.

I gave him the chance to find out when I invited him to join me. To our mutual surprise, he came along. And while I spent much of my time fighting headaches and aching muscles (for some reason it was a difficult fast for me), he tooled along as if nothing were wrong, barely feeling the effects.

---

5 In which of the following situations would you consider fasting? (Check all that apply)

❑ You're unsure how to handle a rebellious child

❑ You are starting or changing a career

❑ You have a lingering illness

❑ You understand a particular theme in Scripture, but it hasn't yet changed your heart

❑ You're concerned about unsaved family members

❑ You can't seem to shake off a persistent sin

❑ You grieve over the nationwide practice of abortion

Typical side effects. If you're unwilling to experience some discomfort, you're not properly prepared to fast. Disciplining our flesh has a price tag attached. But the benefit you'll receive easily outweighs the symptoms that accompany fasting:

Headaches. This may be your body's way of complaining about caffeine withdrawal, or perhaps you're not drinking enough water.

Drowsiness. As your blood sugar levels drop, so does your energy. One time when I was fasting during an unseasonably warm late winter day I lay back in the grass of an open field to pray. I woke up an hour later. Though initially I felt guilty, I realized this was just part of the program. Fasting reminds me how weak I really am.

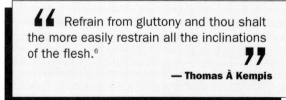

❝ Refrain from gluttony and thou shalt the more easily restrain all the inclinations of the flesh.[6] ❞

— Thomas À Kempis

Lightheadedness. During fasts of more than 24 hours

Meditate on 2 Corinthians 4:16-18.
An eternal perspective makes it much easier to tolerate temporary discomfort.

you may need to move slowly when getting up out of a chair or walking, and you may find it difficult to focus your mind. This symptom usually passes after a day or so.

Stomach cramps. Mild cramps are common, and can be relieved by drinking water. If you are really uncomfortable, drink juice. If the pains are severe, postpone your fast until you can get some medical advice.

Chills. Because your body is not generating as much heat, you'll be especially sensitive to the cold. Wear adequate clothing and have extra blankets for sleeping.

Bad breath. God won't mind, but be sensitive to others around you and use breath mints.

Heightened sense of taste. Tap water may taste terrible to you when you're fasting. Adding lemon slices to your drinking water will take away the metallic taste. On a positive note, your first meal after an extended fast will taste delightful!

Symptoms will vary between individuals. If you fast longer than a few days, many of these side effects would disappear until weeks later, when your body would actually begin to starve.

> **66** Remember that your fast is a privilege, not an obligation. It is the acceptance of a divine invitation to experience [God's] grace in a special way.[7] **99**
>
> — **Donald Whitney**

Ending a fast. The longer your stomach has gone without food, the longer you should take when easing back into a regular eating schedule. A friend of mine phases out of extended fasts by sucking on orange slices one day, drinking broth the next, moving to fresh fruits and vegetables next and only gradually resuming his regular diet. Though this won't be necessary when concluding a shorter fast, avoid the temptation to stuff yourself. You'll regret it.

Finally, finish your fast with thanksgiving. Review the things God has shown you and make specific plans to respond. Having paid the price, take pains to secure your investment.

All the spiritual disciplines require some form of self-denial. Fasting is probably the most notable in this regard. As with any investment in life, be it investing money or investing in physical exercise, the rewards come later. If your experience is anything like mine has been, you'll be surprised at how little investment yields such great rewards through the discipline of seeking God in fasting. ■

1. Who is more deserving of God's grace: A badly overweight couch potato or a highly disciplined, two-fasts-per-week Pharisee?

2. What would be the hardest thing for you to surrender to God?

3. Were you surprised by what you learned about fasting in this chapter?

4. Has anyone in the group had experiences with fasting, either positive or negative?

5. Are you willing to undergo the discomfort of fasting? Did you know what you were getting into when you accepted Christ as Lord?

6. If our fasting doesn't earn God's attention to our prayers, how do you explain the fact that fasting makes our praying more effective?

7. Are you currently facing any situations that would warrant a period of fasting?

RECOMMENDED READING *God's Chosen Fast* by Arthur Wallis (Fort Washington, PA: Christian Literature Crusade, 1968)

Spiritual Disciplines for the Christian Life by Donald S. Whitney (Colorado Springs, CO: NavPress, 1991)

Answer to Warm-Up
(from page 53): According to 1985-86 statistics, the average American consumes 1919.2 pounds of grain annually—more than three times the world average. (This includes indirect consumption of grain fed to livestock and poultry.)

CONFESSION: DOORWAY TO LIFE

JOHN LOFTNESS

SCRIPTURE TEXT   James 5:13-16

WARM-UP   What percentage of those scheduled to stand trial plead guilty in hope of a lighter sentence?

	Felonies	Misdemeanors
A.	29%	34%
B.	43%	51%
C.	57%	65%
D.	72%	83%
E.	88%	94%

(See page 75 for answers)

PERSONAL STUDY   "This is embarrassing, but I believe I should tell you…"

"I thought you should know…"

"I'm ashamed to admit it but…"

Confession of sin is a painful discipline. It's also a doorway to life. If we fail to use this door, we'll find ourselves stumbling around in the deceitfulness of our own souls.

Scripture tells us to confess our sins to God and other people. Though this study will focus almost exclusively on person-to-person confession, we must begin by noting that transparency before God is essential. Without confessing our sins to God, we have no access to his saving and sanctifying grace. And while an initial confession of sin must accompany our conversion, it is also to be the ongoing practice of every child of God. "If we confess our sins," the apostle John noted, "he is faithful and just and will forgive us our sins and purify us from all unrighteousness. If we claim we have not sinned, we make him out to be a liar and his word has no place in our lives" (1Jn 1:9-10).

In general, practicing the spiritual disciplines covered in this book is more difficult in private than in public. Fasting, praying, or studying the Bible as part of a group is far easier than doing those things alone. Confession is a different matter. I have always found it easier to confess my sins to God than to another person. Why? Perhaps because I know God is omniscient and that his love for me is perfect. Consequently, he already knows what I've done before I admit it to him, and I know he'll respond in love, even in his correction. (People, on the other hand, are not as dependable.) I also know God will correct me whether I confess or not, so the sooner I get it out the better.

If I were fully aware of God's holiness, my attitude toward confession might be different. I am the first to admit I have an inadequate fear of the Lord. I long to grow to the place where the sting of shame affects me more when I confess my sins to God than when I confess those same sins to my friends. But I'm not there yet, and in the meantime I've found that confessing to my brothers and sisters increases my fear of God and helps me grow in obedience.

For Further Study:
Read Proverbs 1:7 and Hebrews 10:19-22. What is the balance between fearing God and being confident of his grace?

Before we move on to the practice of this discipline, note that there is one occasion when confession to others is mandatory: when we've offended them. "If you are offering your gift at the altar and there remember that your brother has something against you, leave your gift there in front of the altar. First go and be reconciled to your brother; then come and offer your gift" (Mt 5:23-24). When we've lied or gossiped or expressed anger to someone, we have an obligation to God and to that person to go quickly, admit our wrong, and make appropriate restitution.

---

1 What would make you most nervous about confessing a sin to a Christian friend?

❑ Fear that confessing my sin would give it additional power over me

❑ Fear that my friend would not understand

❑ Fear that I would be asked to leave the church

❑ Fear that I would be embarrassed

❑ Fear that my friend would publish the details of my confession in the church newsletter

❑ Other _____

Six Arguments for Accountability

Confession may be initially painful, but it's also a gift to us. Not only does it glorify God, but it helps us in numerous ways. The following are things that should motivate us to confess our sins to others.

We overcome relational barriers. Sin ruins relationships. When we sin against someone, feelings of resentment or guilt often create a sense of alienation that can only be removed through confession. But confession isn't limited to those we've offended or hurt. By acknowledging our failings to certain people who are close friends in our journey through life, we gain the benefits of accountability *and* a deeper friendship.

> **"** Confession alone makes *deep* fellowship possible, and the lack of it explains much of the superficial quality so commonly found in our church associations.[1] **"**
> — **Dallas Willard**

I won't say it's easy. It's not unusual for me to fear anger, rejection, or disrespect when I confess certain sins to my friends. Yet invariably I hear things like, "I respect you for telling me"…"Now *I'm* convicted of the same thing"…"How can I help you to avoid that in the future?" Transparency builds trust and a depth of understanding. Close relationships are impossible without it.

We overcome fear of rejection. "I always thought that if people knew about my struggles, they'd kick me out of the church." As a pastor, I've heard this refrain more times than I'd like to remember. Often I've responded by saying, "Shame for your sin and the humility of your confession demonstrate that you desire to grow. That's all God requires and that's all we require. This entire church is made up of people who struggle with sin in one form or another. The only people whom God allows us (actually commands us) to reject are those who, after repeated entreaty, *refuse* to admit to or turn from clearly defined sin."

Shame makes us want to reject ourselves, feel as if God has rejected us, and fear the rejection of other godly people. Confession to God frees us from shame, and confession to other believers confirms to us that his forgiveness and acceptance are real. Jesus founded his Church as the place where such transparency and resulting growth can effectively take place. We need encouragement, encouragement, encouragement to overcome sin, and that encouragement comes through confession.

Meditate on 1 John 4:17-18. What frees us from the fear of God's punishment?

2 As you're reading the newspaper one day, you learn about an upcoming television exposé called "The Secret Sins of the Saints"…featuring *your* private life! What one scene would you most want to edit?

(Rather than writing your answer, simply confess it to God, then meditate on his complete acceptance and forgiveness.)

We overcome condemnation. Condemnation results from thoughts or feelings of God's rejection. Whether they are aware of it or not, those apart from Christ live in a perpetual state of condemnation. But an instantaneous change occurs at the point of salvation. According to Paul, condemnation and union with Christ are mutually exclusive (Ro 8:1). It's impossible for one who truly believes to experience God's condemnation.

For Further Study: The more we understand God's infinite mercy, the less Satan's accusations affect us. Read the extraordinary promise in Micah 7:18-19. Also read Jeremiah 31, realizing that the first 30 chapters speak almost exclusively of Israel's sin and coming judgment.

Yet at times, for different reasons, we still feel condemned. Some of us, in our pride or ignorance, develop an unbiblical notion that our behavior determines our status before our loving God. Others are susceptible to the accusations of our ancient enemy, Satan, who roams the earth looking for people to condemn. Still others have an overly sensitive conscience. While not feeling God's *rejection*, they constantly expect his displeasure over any and every perceived misstep. Their problem often stems from a misunderstanding of the nature of sin (which is too broad a topic for this study). They can get help by confessing their sins to someone with a healthy conscience and a strong grasp of what the Scriptures say about sin.

One of the ironies of Martin Luther's life can be seen in his relationship with a young follower and brilliant theologian, Philip Melancthon. Before coming to an understanding of justification by faith, Luther would spend up to six hours at a time confessing—in excruciating detail—every thought and feeling that he considered sin. His confessor, Johanan von Staupitz, saw such confession as the inner workings of a potentially insane man and suggested that Luther go out and "commit a real sin" so he could then have something genuine to confess.

Years later, with Luther now the leader of the reform movement in Germany, Melancthon would come to him with his own lengthy list of supposed sins. Luther apparently had less patience with Melancthon than his mentor von Staupitz had with him, but he gave facetious counsel similar to that of von Staupitz: "Sin for all you are worth," he told the conscience-pained scholar. "God can forgive only a lusty sinner."[2] Certainly, Luther was not encouraging a breach of the Ten Commandments, but chiding the young reformer to reform his own conscience. Some of us need to hear the same.

As a pastor I hear many confessions of sin. Often the person's burden remains even after genuinely repenting. One of the most fulfilling things I do is to affirm the reality of God's absolute forgiveness. People seem to get great assurance from just hearing, "You've confessed your sin to God. You've asked him to forgive you. He does forgive you. Now stop walking in condemnation and accept what Jesus did for you on the cross." Through confession we open the door so that others can jolt us out of condemnation with a clear, biblical perspective.

> The discipline of confession brings an end to pretense. God is calling into being a Church that can openly confess its frail humanity and know the forgiving and empowering graces of Christ. Honesty leads to confession, and confession leads to change.[3]
>
> **— Richard Foster**

---

3 How sensitive is your conscience? Make an "X" at the appropriate point on the scale below.

| **Seared** | **Sensitive** |
| no twinge of remorse | feel guilty about everything |

We overcome pride. Not everybody struggles with a hypersensitive conscience. In fact, some of us have a hard time recognizing that we really have sinned. The Spirit's conviction shouts at us from loudspeakers and we think he's paging someone else.

Blame-shifting is one of the most subtle forms of pride. It can derail us from moving forward in our relationship with God and leave us in a train wreck if we let it invade other areas of our lives. Husbands excuse their indulgence in lust by blaming their unloving wives. Wives blame their bitterness on their preoccupied, insensitive husbands. In confessing our sins and struggles, we can get help from someone with a clear view of sin who's willing to shatter our pride and boldly call sin for what it is.

Meditate on Proverbs 28:13. Have you ever tried to hide your sin, either from God or your friends? What did it feel like?

Long ago my friend Gary and I agreed to be transparent with each other. When I know that my sin is more that a small, temporary stumble or that I'm experiencing repeated temptation in the same area, we talk. I feel embarrassed when I admit my sins and weaknesses, but in humbling myself there comes an openness to experiencing God's grace for the battle.

We overcome sickness. The book of James makes this intriguing appeal: "Therefore confess your sins to each other and pray for each other so that you may be healed" (Jas 5:16). Although most commentators are quick to qualify this verse, narrowing it to a wholeness of the soul, the relationship between confession and physical healing is hard to dismiss. Confession may not always lead to healing, and healing may not always be denied apart from confession. When we sin, though, our conscience is stained. In this sense, I think it's fair to say that sin makes our souls sick. As we confess our sins to one another, we can pray that our bad conscience and any weakness or defect it has brought into our minds, hearts, or bodies will be healed and made whole. Flushing out the soul through confession is an excellent first step toward physical healing.

We overcome the enemy through effective prayer. If we refuse to confess our sins to others, their ability to pray for us is quite limited. They may not even be aware of the spiritual battle raging inside us. As James suggests, confession doesn't merely result in a little encouragement and a slap on the back. It empowers the prayers of the saints on our behalf. Like a trumpet blown in battle, confession rallies others to our side in a united assault against the enemy. But if we're too proud to cry out for help, we'll find ourselves fighting alone.

Who Should Know?

As Philip Melancthon learned from Martin Luther, not all sins are worth sharing with others. Most of our daily, non-habitual sins can be adequately handled in our confession to God. Don't feel you have to call your pastor each time you lose your temper or envy someone's new car.

In fact, the Bible doesn't give us any rules regarding confession. That didn't stop the early Church from developing rules of her own, but we're not bound to these man-made traditions. No one has any biblical authority to impose on you a certain pattern of confession.

An absence of specific guidelines leaves some people

For Further Study:
To appreciate the way the early Christians relied on each other's prayers, see Ro 15:30-32; 2Co 1:10-11; Col 4:12.

Meditate on Colossians 2:8.
Unless they reinforce and are supported by biblical truth, religious traditions have no value. Is there any area where such a tradition is holding you "captive"?

feeling perplexed: "Do I need to confess this or not? What if I don't? What if I do?" John Calvin concluded that the spiritual discipline of confession should be a voluntary practice: "Confession of this nature ought to be free, so as not to be exacted of all, but only recommended to those who feel they have need of it. And even those who use it according to their necessity must neither be compelled by any precept nor artfully induced to enumerate all their sins, only insofar that they should deem it for their interest that they may obtain the full benefit of consolation." Here's a modern-day paraphrase: If in your desire to please God you think confessing to someone else would be helpful, go ahead.

> " The confession of evil works is the first beginning of good works.[4] "
>
> — **Augustine of Hippo**

Confession is always called for when our sins negatively affect others. Our biblical responsibility, as we read earlier, is to go to those we've offended and ask forgiveness. Even if they don't respond, we must obey God. Confession is also a powerful tool for overcoming repeated sins. If your fear of God fails to keep you away from habitual sin, add the fear of your friends! The inevitability of an embarrassing confession may be just the incentive you need to walk purely before God and man.

Finally, confession is essential in cases of serious sin. Because of the ramifications of something like child abuse, fornication, or stealing, you would be foolish to confess only to God. In this last case someone with pastoral gifts and authority would be best suited to help you walk through the consequences of your actions.

Meditate on Psalm 32. Does this make you eager to practice the spiritual discipline of confession?

4 In which of the following areas would you benefit most from being accountable to a trusted friend?

❑ Work habits

❑ Spiritual disciplines

❑ Finances

❑ Sexual purity

❑ Self-control (diet, anger, exercise, TV)

❑ Taming the tongue

❑ Other _____

If confessing our sins to a brother or sister is normal for us, we'll rarely or never have to go to a pastor. The circle of confession needn't exceed the circle of the sin's impact except for the purposes of accountability and care. However, we are obligated to confess to anyone who has been affected by our sin.

Confession will make you very vulnerable, so it pays to be selective. Find someone who listens carefully and withholds counsel until he fully understands the situation. Find someone compassionate who will keep your confession in confidence. Find someone who will not abuse your trust by making unbiblical demands. Also, though you'll want to confess to someone with a big heart, make sure that individual has a healthy view of sin. Avoid anyone who will react in horror to your confession or, at the other end of the spectrum, will smother you in mercy when you need rebuke. We'll get the most benefit when we confess to someone who accepts us without being shocked by our sin, yet helps us confront the seriousness of what we've done to God and others.

> 66 A man who confesses his sins in the presence of a brother knows that he is no longer alone with himself; he experiences the presence of God in the reality of the other person. As long as I am by myself in the confession of my sins everything remains in the dark, but in the presence of a brother the sin has to be brought into the light.[5] 99
>
> — **Dietrich Bonhoeffer**

Wisdom dictates that we take two final precautions with confession. If your sin is of a sexual nature, don't confess to a member of the opposite sex. That's inappropriate and unwise. It has the potential of getting you in deeper trouble and of tempting the other person. And beware of confessing something that releases you but hurts someone else in the process. Telling a friend you've struggled to accept her personality may destroy her remaining self-confidence. Telling your spouse you find someone else more attractive will only cause hurt. When these kinds of situations arise, confide in someone who won't be rocked by your confession.

The Signs of True Confession

Whether you're confessing to someone or hearing a confession, it's important to know the genuine from the counterfeit. Authentic confession will be characterized by the following:

It is specific. The offender need not give every gory, morbid detail, but enough to clarify the nature of the sin. It's not going to accomplish God's purpose merely to say, "Pray for me—I'm struggling with anger."

It includes motive. Sinful actions often represent just the smoke spewing out of the volcano; what's more important is what's going on with the magma beneath the mountain. Perhaps you lied about your level of education the first time you introduced yourself to a friend. What motivated you to do that? Pride? A fear of rejection? A sinful love of approval? Confession should go to the heart of the issue. If you desire to change, the "why" must factor as prominently in your confession as the "what."

It is sorrowful. There's a huge difference between admitting you were wrong and feeling remorse about your wrong. I have confronted people who blithely said, "Oh, yeah, I'm sorry." That's not the stuff of which effective confessions are made. Rather, while making sure we don't slip into condemnation, we should grieve over the pain our sin has caused others, especially God.

For Further Study:
Read 2 Corinthians 7:5-11. What's the difference between godly sorrow and worldly sorrow?

In yielding to his lust for Bathsheba, David committed both murder and adultery. He killed Uriah and widowed Bathsheba. His actions led to the death of his illegitimate son. Surprisingly, though, his confession in Psalm 51 focuses exclusively on God: "Against you, you only, have I sinned and done what is evil in your sight." While David's example doesn't absolve us from responsibility to get things right with others, his perspective fosters a healthy fear of God and a deeper sorrow over sin.

---

5 Read David's confession in Psalm 51:4 again. Do you think he was denying the harm he had done to others, or did he just have a different view of sin's consequences? Briefly explain your answer.

It is accompanied by repentance. Confession is not genuine apart from a determination to live one's life differently. The person confessing sin should be able to describe specific, measurable changes that have been or will be implemented.

It is made in light of the Cross. The wording could be completely different, but here's the idea: "God, I confess this sin before you. I ask, Father, that you would count this under Jesus' payment on the cross, and I realize this sin participated in nailing him to the cross."

It is followed by intercessory prayer. As we've already seen in James, prayer is the perfect follow-up to confession. It moves us out of the negative (confessing our past failure) and into the positive (requesting God's success in the future).

It results in an experience of forgiveness. As Calvin said, the goal of confession is consolation, not condemnation. The spiritual discipline of confession releases us into the joy of forgiveness. It cleans our conscience. It makes us whole and gives us fresh power to live like Jesus.

"No discipline seems pleasant at the time, but painful," wrote the author of Hebrews. "Later on, however, it produces a harvest of righteousness and peace for those who have been trained by it" (Heb 12:11). Yes, confession is a painful discipline, but it is a discipline that leads to life. ■

THE SEVEN A's OF CONFESSION

In his book *The Peacemaker*, Ken Sande teaches how to pursue reconciliation with those with whom we have conflict. His "Seven A's of Confession" address confessing sin to a person you've sinned against, but the principles are helpful for any confession, including our sins against God:

1. Address everyone involved.
2. Avoid "If..." "But..." "Maybe..."
3. Admit specifically.
4. Apologize—express sorrow or regret.
5. Accept the consequences.
6. Alter your behavior.
7. Ask for forgiveness.[6]

---

1. Do you find it hard to accept God's forgiveness? Why?

2. Have you had (or heard of) any bad experiences with accountability?

3. What's the value of confessing something to others that we have already confessed to God?

4. Read 1 John 1:5-10. How does confession to God and others help us "walk in the light"?

5. What are the most effective ways you have found to battle condemnation?

6. Is spoken confession any better than silent confession?

7. Would anything prevent you from singling out a stubborn sin and confessing it to a trusted friend?

RECOMMENDED READING *The Peacemaker* by Ken Sande (Grand Rapids, MI: Baker Book House, 1991)

Answers to Warm-Up
(from page 65): Statistics for this question were provided by a State Attorney's office in a major urban judicial district. In the case of both felonies and misdemeanors the answer is (E): 88% and 94%, respectively, of those indicted enter a guilty plea rather than face trial.

SOLITUDE: GETTING ALONE WITH GOD

JOHN LOFTNESS

SCRIPTURE TEXT 1 Kings 19:1-18

WARM-UP How much sleep does the average adult need per night?

A. Five hours or less
B. Six hours
C. Seven hours
D. Eight hours
E. More than eight hours

(See page 88 for answer)

PERSONAL STUDY "Elijah was a man just like us" (Jas 5:17).

I find this statement one of the more difficult in the Bible to accept. Elijah was anything but normal. We know little of his background except for his hometown, Tishbe, an obscure place in biblical geography. He arrives suddenly on the scene during a time of national apostasy in Israel's history and announces a three-year drought that will only end when he says so.

Though lots of people even in our day have announced the end of the world, none have been accurate to date. Such people usually make their announcement to a select few believers who are promised they will escape the calamities to come. That wasn't Elijah's style. He spoke directly to his king, a man named Ahab. In effect he prophesied economic disaster and claimed that it was under his control. The prophecy proved true and Elijah, along with all of Israel, suffered through the drought. For this the prophet became nationally infamous and was given the nickname "The Troubler of Israel."

At the end of three years Elijah received word from God to announce to Ahab the end of the drought. At the time, Ahab's wife Jezebel, a Baal worshiper and daughter of the king of Sidon, was committing genocide against the prophets of the Lord. Ahab was out looking for him when Elijah reappeared. Rather than fleeing for his life, Elijah tells Ahab to gather Jezebel's pagan prophets and meet him on Mount Carmel for a showdown. Ahab complies, probably because he was desperate for rain.

The story is familiar. Four hundred and fifty prophets of Baal spend half the day screaming, chanting, dancing, and finally slashing themselves with swords and spears in a desperate attempt to get their god to consume a sacri-ficed bull with fire from heaven. In the end, it doesn't work. Elijah, who had a flair for making his point, has gallons of water poured on the dead bull and his pyre, prays a simple prayer, and watches as the Lord of heaven and earth incinerates the bull, the wood, the stone altar, the water, and the earth beneath it . The audience decides that if anybody deserves their support at this time it is Elijah and his God. The prophets of Baal are thus summarily slain. Elijah then proceeds to tell Ahab that rain is on its way.

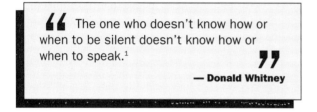

The one who doesn't know how or when to be silent doesn't know how or when to speak.[1]

— Donald Whitney

Not bad for a day's work.

Following events like these, one would expect Elijah to command Ahab to repent of his apostasy, execute or at least banish his queen, and cleanse the land of idols and their worship. Then Ahab could live and rule happily-ever-after with Elijah as his trusted adviser.

The opposite happens. A drenched Ahab crawls back to Samaria to report the day's events. In a fit of rage, Jezebel invokes the curse of her gods on herself if she hasn't killed Elijah in the coming 24 hours. So what does this commander of rain and fire, this slayer of apostates do? He runs to the desert for his life. Why? Because he was a man just like us. He could only take so much. After three years of drought, hiding, and infamy—followed by a day of tense confrontation and massive bloodshed—he'd had it. He could take no more. He was terrified of this venomous queen, despite the fact that he had seen her prophets deci-sively defeated only the day before.

This kind of collapse can happen to anyone who seeks to serve God. We end up drained and can give no more. The slightest pressure, let alone a death threat, causes us to fall apart. Elijah was so overwhelmed that he sat in the desert and prayed a suicide prayer: "I have had enough, Lord," he said, "Take my life; I am no better than my ancestors." So what did God do? First he met Elijah's need for food, then he sent him to a mountain where he could be refreshed alone with his Lord. God gave him food, God gave him rest, and God gave him solitude. In solitude Elijah was able to regain the strength and the vision to once again serve his God.

God Doesn't Shout

I don't know of any "how to" books that recommend hibernating in a mountaintop cave as a way to beat depression. Modern-day counselors probably would have urged Elijah to try anti-depression medication, join a recovery group, or perhaps build up his weakened self-esteem through positive mental images. But God had a simpler and more effective plan: get away, get alone, and get quiet.

Before speaking to Elijah on the mountaintop, God sent a violent wind, an earthquake, and then a fire. As awesome as these were—not to mention noisy—God wasn't in them. Elijah didn't even come out of his cave until he heard the sound of a gentle whisper. That was his cue. And that's when the Lord began speaking.

> **❝** It is important that we get still to wait on God. And it is best that we get alone, preferably with our Bible outspread before us. Then if we will we may draw near to God and begin to hear Him speak to us in our hearts.[2] **❞**
>
> — **A.W. Tozer**

We don't hear God in the earthquake, in the fire, in the violent rushing wind— we hear him in a whisper. That's tough for us living in the noisiest era of world history. With television, radio, telephones, email, newspapers, billboards, and more clamoring for our attention, we would certainly find it a lot easier to hear God if he cranked heaven's loudspeakers up to full volume. But that's not his style. He won't yank away the headphones of your personal stereo system or turn down your car radio to get your attention. He whispers. And we can't hear his whisper unless we're quiet inside.

When we find ourselves in Elijah's shoes, needing a fresh perspective on life or new hope for what the future holds, it's time to seek out a quiet place where we can be alone with God.

1 A brand-new Christian comes to you expressing frustration about the difficulty of hearing God's voice. "Why is God so quiet?" he demands. Pick one of the following as your response:

❏ The ozone layer muffles the sound of God's voice

❏ God developed an eternal case of laryngitis after speaking audibly to Jesus while he was on earth

❏ Man's ear wax thickened after Adam and Eve's sin

❏ If God did anything but whisper, we would be blown into the next state

❏ God is unwilling to impose his thoughts on us. He reveals himself to those who diligently seek him.

For Further Study:
Silence is a mark of wisdom, as Solomon states in Pr 10:19, Pr 17:28, and Ecc 9:17.

I seem to feel a greater need for solitude than most people. There's a path along the Potomac River where I enjoy walking. More often than not the noisiest thing I hear is a woodpecker. Sometimes I pray; sometimes I'm just quiet. I don't always hear anything unique from God. Yet my goal is to create opportunities where I would be able to hear him if he had something to say. Unless I routinely break out of my noisy, busy lifestyle, I'm not sure God would be able to get a word in edgewise. So I've made solitude a discipline.

At times we just need to be by ourselves. Jesus felt that need when he got news John the Baptist had been beheaded. Matthew writes, "When Jesus heard what had happened, he withdrew by boat privately to a solitary place" (Mt 14:13). Imagine our Lord's emotions. John was his cousin. This was his forerunner, the man who understood his messianic mission better than anyone else. And what an ugly reminder that his own death was imminent! It's my guess that after such discouraging news Jesus needed to get refocused on his ministry and gain fresh strength from his Father.

Maybe you're confused about God's purpose for your life. Maybe you're grieving over the death of a loved one, or are stressed out by the demands at work. Perhaps you have young children and your brain is fried from a million and one questions like, "Why does the toaster make the toast brown?" It's time to get alone with God. Find a quiet time and place to wait for his words.

Scripture doesn't command solitude. You can be a Christian without taking long walks by the river or holing up in a mountaintop cave. But if you hope to hear God's voice and have your spirit replenished, you will definitely want to explore the benefits of spending extended time alone with God. Learn what makes your life noisy, then block out seasons of solitude when you can silence those things and focus on your Father.

> ❝ The normal course of day-to-day human interactions locks us into patterns of feeling, thought, and action that are geared to a world set against God. Nothing but solitude can allow the development of a freedom from the ingrained behaviors that hinder our integration into God's order.[3] ❞
>
> — **Dallas Willard**

---

2 Because we often depend on noise to block out turmoil in our hearts, solitude can be scary. Briefly describe your thoughts on the following quote by Louis Bouyer: "Solitude...serves to crack open and burst apart the shell of our superficial securities."[4]

Personal Retreats

Meditate on Proverbs 16:3. What is involved in committing our plans to the Lord? Do you submit decisions to him for his "rubber stamp" approval or do you let him lead you to a decision?

Soon after submitting my life to God as a teenager, I discovered the value of spending extended time with God on "personal retreats." It's never easy to set aside a day or several days for this purpose, but these large chunks of solitude have been such a benefit that I can no longer live without them. They restore my spirit, they deepen my intercession, and I frequently receive specific direction from God for problems or decisions I'm facing.

Now even if you agree with me in theory, you probably have lots of questions—the what, where, when, and why questions that are essential in order to fully understand how personal retreats work. I'll do my best to answer those questions over the next few pages.

It would be great if the Bible recorded the specifics of our Lord's retreats. We know he spent a good deal of time in solitude, and that those times contributed to his phenomenal spiritual strength. But he apparently didn't publish an agenda or itinerary. So the most I can offer are my own experiences and suggestions. They will be practical, but they'll also be mine, and so obviously not Scripture. If other techniques make your solitude more fruitful, please don't feel there's anything sacred about mine.

Choosing a time. If an urgent need emerges, there's no time like the present for taking a retreat. Yet by making retreats a routine part of our schedule, we can potentially catch some problems before they turn into crises. One model would be to set aside three or four hours each month; one day every three months; and two or three days once a year. Maybe you can't commit this much time. Maybe you're in a season where you need to commit more. Whatever the case, I would encourage you to see retreats as a preemptive strike rather than an emergency escape.

Picking the place. Atmosphere is critical for an effective time with God. Here are some important criteria for choosing the best location:

> 66 Some are greatly affected when in company; but have nothing that bears any manner of proportion to it in secret, in close meditation, prayer and conversing with God when alone and separated from the world. A true Christian doubtless delights in religious fellowship and Christian conversation, and finds much to affect his heart in it; but he also delights at times to retire from all mankind, to converse with God in solitude. And this also has peculiar advantages for fixing his heart, and engaging his affections. True religion disposes persons to be much alone in solitary places for holy meditation and prayer.[5] 99
>
> — Jonathan Edwards

A quiet place with few distractions. I wouldn't recommend going to the local shopping mall. Also, make sure you get away from the pressures of your daily routine. Rather than taking retreats at home, my wife will use the home of a friend who is on vacation. That way she isn't tempted to clean the closets or reorganize the bookcase.

A safe place. Women especially should find a place where their efforts to seek God won't be hindered by fear or danger. If being alone in a strange place makes you nervous, consider taking your retreats with a friend.

A place with adequate heat. Once your teeth start chattering, your brain will have a hard time focusing on God.

Fasting makes you especially susceptible to the cold. Unless it's the middle of the summer, take along extra clothes and blankets—a space heater is great in the winter—just to insure that you stay warm.

A place with adequate space. I enjoy doing a lot of walking during my personal retreats. I'd probably get cabin fever if I were shut up in a hotel room for more than a few hours. So I've gone to a nearby retreat center that has over 200 acres of land, including a path that goes all around the property. This lets me enjoy God's creation and get a little exercise as I think and pray.

A place where I can be loud without disturbing anyone. I have difficulty focusing on God for long stretches of time. If on my retreat I find a National Geographic magazine that someone left on a shelf, I can easily waste a couple of hours. Sometimes what began as a time of prayer ends with me mentally planning our next vacation. One of my most effective weapons against distraction is to sing and pray out loud. But that's hard to do when you're worrying that any moment someone is going to bang on your door or wall.

A place that has minimal temptations. By using a little common sense we can spare ourselves some needless temptation—and potentially, shame. Men should take extra precautions. A condo overlooking a beach full of sunbathers will be problematic. I personally don't like hotel rooms because the television is so prominent, and in-room pornographic movies are common fare, let alone the other junk that comes over the cable.

Now maybe you have Christlike levels of self-control. That's great. But a personal retreat is no time to test your immunity to temptation. When we are alone our flesh and the Devil can seem to work especially hard to undermine this time with God.

 Write down one or two places where you could take an effective personal retreat.

For Further Study:
Use a concordance to find the passages in Psalms where shouting is an expression of worship. You can begin with Ps 20:5, 33:3, and 35:27.

Meditate on 1 Peter 5:8-9. Though the enemy is no match for our King, we must not underestimate his ability to harm and distract us.

Meditate on James 1:5-8. What promise motivates us to seek God's wisdom? What is the prerequisite?

A place that is inexpensive. A friend's house or retreat center may not have all the amenities of a hotel, but they are much easier on the budget. If you are the outdoors type, consider camping. On one retreat, I paid just five dollars for a site at a nearby campground. Equipped with my tent, card table, chair, and all the water I could drink, I had a great time with God.

Plan in advance. Before leaving for your retreat, you should have a clear idea of what you hope to accomplish. Otherwise, you will find yourself drifting aimlessly through the time and wondering at the end whether it was worthwhile.

What are your reasons for taking a retreat: getting God's guidance about a job offer? studying a book on personal finances? breaking out of a spiritual rut? Put your goals in writing. Make them as specific as possible. Also, break them down into categories:

- Situations/people requiring prayer
- Decisions requiring an answer
- Issues requiring study

You may need to do some preliminary research in order to accomplish certain goals during your retreat. For example, if you will be seeking biblical guidelines for more effective time management, do a two-week time study before you take your retreat. This way you can work with something concrete.

---

4 *Well, I really would love to take a personal retreat, but...*

❑ My hamster's emotions are especially fragile right now; I'm not sure she could live without me

❑ I'm expecting an urgent call from Great-Uncle Zeke

❑ My annual bonus depends on my working every weekend for the next 51 weeks

❑ I'm studying grace right now, and don't want to do anything legalistic

❑ I promised to serve my wife by oiling the door hinges

Give some real thought to the items you will need during your retreat. It's frustrating to arrive and find that you forgot a blanket or the book you had planned to study. I often bring a lot more study materials than I expect to cover, and then try to discipline myself so that I only look at the things that truly meet my needs.

If you are going on a retreat with another person, sit down and discuss your expectations in advance. Plan the times you will spend together and alone. Do everything you can to prevent misunderstandings from occurring during your retreat.

Schedule your time. If you've never taken a personal retreat, 24 hours may seem like eternity. But the time passes quickly, so keep your expectations realistic. If you go away hoping to read five books on parenting, you will come back totally discouraged because you only got through the first half of the first one.

Also, set up a schedule that includes variety. Sometimes I spend my time in prayer and studying the Bible; sometimes I concentrate on planning or seeking God for direction. Sometimes I fast while on retreat; other times I don't. I try to tailor my retreats to best address my current situation.

God doesn't expect you to enter your room, drop to your knees in fervent intercession, and emerge two days later. Rotate your activities to keep things interesting. Allow time for breaks. Scatter your prayer, worship, waiting, planning, and study throughout the day.

An ideal schedule would include sufficient detail but remain flexible. The Holy Spirit may have plans for your retreat that totally surprise you. Once I brought along a book on child training that I had expected to scan briefly. As I got into it, though, God began opening my eyes to how I should be raising my own children and serving the students at the school where I worked. I devoted a significant chunk of that retreat to reading the whole book. Leave God the option of rescheduling your priorities.

Recording your insights. Before ending your retreat, write down the things you have learned. What seemed so vivid and clear during your time of solitude fades quickly once you are again surrounded by noise. Capture it on paper before it escapes.

Don't be surprised if your retreat ends without any significant new insights from God. You might not come away

> 66 Let him who cannot be alone beware of community....Let him who is not in community beware of being alone....Each by itself has profound pitfalls and perils. One who wants fellowship without solitude plunges into the void of words and feelings, and one who seeks solitude without fellowship perishes in the abyss of vanity, self-infatuation, and despair.[6] 99
>
> — **Dietrich Bonhoeffer**

For Further Study:
Read Acts 10:9-48. If Peter had known the surprise God had in store for him, he might not have been motivated to pray that day!

feeling great, but if you're like me, you will come away *satisfied*. There have been times when I don't sense any dramatic direction or insights from God. Time alone with him is enough.

We can be confident, however, that our investment of time will be worthwhile in the long run. The Lord often chooses to speak to me at a later time when I least expect it, reminding me that it is grace—not my spiritual disciplines—that moves him to communicate. If I got answers based on the intensity of my prayers, I'm sure I wouldn't get as many answers as I do!

---

5 Are you 100% confident of God's eagerness to answer your questions and guide your steps? He is more responsive and open than the best teacher you ever had. By way of meditation, use the space below to write out Proverbs 2:1-6.

Rest

The discipline of solitude helps us accomplish one of God's strongest commands: the command to rest. He gave the Fourth Commandment (resting on the Sabbath) more ink than any of the other nine (Ex 20:8-11). Why? Look at the pace of life in the average American household. We act as if our worth is a function of our busyness. Rest—at least in the United States—is almost a dirty word.

Jesus made it clear the Sabbath was made for man, not man for the Sabbath (Mk 2:27). From the epistle to the Colossians we can deduce that the New Testament Church felt no obligation to uphold the Old Testament Sabbath laws (Col 2:16). The Law was fulfilled in Christ. We're not expected to practice Sabbath rest the way the Jews did.

But though their practice had become legalistic, the

For Further Study:
Read Matthew 12:1-14. How did the Jewish religious leaders distort God's original purpose for the Sabbath?

> **"** Technology is increasing the heart-beat. We are inundated with information. The mind can't handle it all. The pace is so fast now, I sometimes feel like a gunfighter dodging bullets.[7] **"**
>
> — **James Trunzo**

principle remains. Rest was God's idea. He spent six days creating the world, then rested on the seventh, and that before he gave any laws. That rhythm of work and rest is still God's ideal for us today. The Soviet Communist Party learned the hard way. They tried to increase productivity by switching from a seven-day week to a ten-day week: nine days at work, one day of rest. Instead of generating more output, though, the workers became far less productive. We work most effectively when we imitate the weekly schedule that God began at creation.

---

6 Which of the following quotes most clearly indicates America's need for rest?[8]

❑ "I do things in a lot of 3-1/2-minute segments. Experience just sort of rolls by me."—*Anthropologist Peter Hammond*

❑ "Time may have become the most precious commodity in the land."—*Pollster Louis Harris*

❑ "I gave up pressure for Lent."—*Manhattan theater director*

❑ "My wife and I were sitting on the beach in Anguilla on one of our rare vacations, and even there my staff was able to reach me."—*Architect James Trunzo*

❑ "Tired is my middle name."—*Single mother Carol Rohder*

"What requires more faith," asks Bible teacher Derek Prince, "to work or to rest?" Surprisingly, the latter is usually true. Resting—especially when there's lots of work to do—forces us to depend on God. It reminds us that all our energy and effort are ultimately insufficient. It makes us lean on the invisible rather than relying on the concrete.

It is easy to confuse rest with leisure, but they are not necessarily the same. For example, I enjoy a good football game on TV, but it's not a restful activity for me. I can get tense watching the ever-shifting drama of a close game.

Now there's nothing wrong with watching football, but in order to rest I need to do something recreational—something that "recreates" me. A long nap, a good book, a hike in the woods, or an afternoon with my wife and children are far more effective than the Washington Redskins when it comes to rejuvenating and refreshing my mind and body. Other spiritual disciplines like prayer, meditation, and fasting also help me to slow down and refuel.

> **❝** [I]f we would so take heed to our ways that we sin not with our tongue, we must accustom ourselves much to solitude and silence, and sometimes with the Psalmist, 'Hold our peace even from good,' till once we have gotten some command over that unruly member.[9] **❞**
>
> — **Henry Scougal**

Remember when you were a kid and hated taking naps? You may still find it hard to rest. But you will live a healthier and more productive life if you set aside one day in seven to break the hurried pace of the week and rest. ■

GROUP DISCUSSION

1. If you were locked up in solitary confinement for a month, what would you do to maintain sanity?

2. Does the thought of taking a personal retreat intimidate you?

3. What are the main sources of "noise"—both external and internal—in your life?

4. How do you recognize God's voice when he speaks?

5. The author says we are "living in the noisiest era of world history" (Page 79). What do you think he means by that? Give examples.

6. What training or encouragement would you need in order to feel ready to take a personal retreat?

7. Describe the difference between rest and leisure and give one personal example of each.

8. Where in your weekly schedule could you include a time for solitude? (Start small and work your way up.)

Answer to Warm-Up
(from page 77): According to most authorities, the answer is (D)—eight hours per night. Most adults sleep only six or seven hours a night.

AN APPETITE FOR GOD

C.J. MAHANEY

SCRIPTURE TEXT Matthew 5:6

WARM-UP Which of the following movies posted the greatest box-office sales?

A. *The Lion King*
B. *Independence Day*
C. *E.T. the Extra-Terrestrial*
D. *Forrest Gump*
E. *Jurassic Park*
F. *Home Alone*

(See page 99 for answer)

PERSONAL STUDY For years now—decades, actually—I've enjoyed *Sports Illustrated* every week (except for the deplorable, pandering, exploitative swimsuit issue). When I get the mail on Thursdays, I tend to lose all awareness of the world around me. Time stops. Only something significant like an earthquake or the smell of chocolate could get my attention. I've been known to stand there at the mailbox for long periods of time, oblivious to everything but sports.

One Thursday a few years ago I was walking back from the mailbox, eager to sit down and read the latest issue, when I was interrupted by a clear impression in my spirit. Brief, quiet—but unmistakable. "You want to read that magazine more than my Word," whispered the voice.

My initial reaction was to disagree and dismiss this as an unwarranted guilt trip. But with a sense of grief I recognized that God had spoken. And, as always, he was right.

Slowly, subtly, I had transferred my enthusiasm from God's Word to *Sports Illustrated* and the daily sports page.

It wasn't that I had stopped spending time in the Word and prayer. Those remained consistent. But though my "eating habits" appeared healthy, my spiritual appetite was gone.

Our spiritual appetite is a product of our regeneration. If we don't cultivate that desire, however, it gradually subsides. The result? Individuals who are dull of hearing and no longer pursue God and his purpose with the same intensity. They may be as faithful as ever in serving and attending meetings, but they're no longer hearing God's voice. They maintain the principles, but no longer experience God's presence.

Most of us are very aware of our physical appetites. So are advertisers. Even if I've just gotten up from the dinner table, a seafood commercial can instantly make me hungry all over again. And when I'm at the local mall, the smell wafting out of Mrs. Field's Cookies is devastating. Thirst works the same way—a hard game of basketball or a jalapeno pepper creates a serious need. At least three times a day I'm in touch with my physical appetites, or they are in touch with me.

But our spiritual appetites are less demanding. My soul doesn't rumble and growl the way my stomach does when empty. Also, I can find myself deceived into assuming I have some vast, endless reserve of spiritual strength which will sustain me indefinitely. With that mindset, I could be suffering from spiritual malnutrition and not even know it.

Symptoms of Disease

In Matthew 5:6, Jesus provides us with a thermometer for checking our spiritual health: "Blessed are those who hunger and thirst for righteousness, for they will be filled." Let's be honest. How is your spiritual appetite at present? Are your devotions characterized by the intense desire Jesus describes in this verse? Has the past year seen an increase or decrease in your appetite for God, his presence, his righteousness, and his Word?

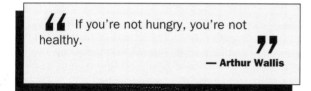

❝ If you're not hungry, you're not healthy. **❞**

— Arthur Wallis

This exercise is not meant to condemn or provoke legalistic introspection (although it *is* meant to convict, where needed). God loves and accepts us on the basis of Christ's finished work—period. Then, having laid a solid foundation of justification by grace through faith, God desires that we press on to develop our relationship with him. Just as we

Meditate on Psalm 42:1-2. Imagine the extreme thirst described here. Is it possible that you could experience such an intense longing for God?

submit to periodic medical exams to check our physical health, we need to monitor our spiritual health at regular intervals. Loss of appetite, whether physical or spiritual, is symptomatic of disease. And where our hearts are involved, it is a "disease" that hides itself very well.

---

1 What are your vital signs? Use this self-diagnostic test to check your spiritual health.
(H=Healthy, Q=Questionable, S=Sick)

	H	Q	S
Heart (Pr 4:23)	❏	❏	❏
Eyes (Ps 123:1-2; Heb 12:2)	❏	❏	❏
Ears (Pr 2:1-2; Is 50:4)	❏	❏	❏
Lungs (Ps 150:6)	❏	❏	❏
Blood pressure (Php 4:6-7)	❏	❏	❏
Oral hygiene (Jas 3:3-10)	❏	❏	❏
Hand-eye coordination (Jas 2:14-17)	❏	❏	❏
Body odor (2Co 2:14-16)	❏	❏	❏

If your hunger has subsided, it is imperative that you seek God's diagnosis and make whatever changes are necessary—no matter how drastic. Your condition requires immediate care.

As you seek God, he may reveal a specific sin. (If so, deal with it radically.) But often you will find that what has decreased your hunger and thirst for righteousness is a normally innocent activity, a typically harmless pastime. It's not inherently evil, but it has *become* an evil for us, because we have allowed it to take too high a priority in our lives. We have adopted it as an idol, and the Lord himself is no longer our passion and priority. Instead, we spend our limited time and energy in the worship of false gods. Yet our God is a jealous God who will specifically confront anything that affects our passion for him.

The Scripture says, "let us throw off everything that hinders and the sin that so easily entangles…" (He 12:1). In the next section we will look at some of the more subtle hindrances Christians often encounter. Prepare yourself to be challenged. And purpose in your heart now that nothing—absolutely nothing—will dull your appetite for God.

For Further Study: When young King Josiah discovered and studied God's Word, he took radical action against Judah's idolatrous practices (2Ki 22:1-23:25). If the Holy Spirit revealed idols in your life, would you be willing to follow Josiah's lead?

Time Bandits

The development of your spiritual life should take precedence over all else. If something is important to us, our schedules will reflect that, and a close look at how we spend our time is a sure indication of what we have built our lives around. So if we are not taking the necessary time to pursue God via the spiritual disciplines, it simply means some other activity has become more important to us.

Here are some of the activities which most frequently compete with what could otherwise be spiritually productive time:

Television. I can almost hear the groans. You don't need me to tell you that Christians should exercise great care in choosing what we watch on TV. But it's equally important to monitor *how much* we watch. For many of you, television is more of a habit than you would like to admit (and if you can't admit it, you won't change it).

It takes time to cultivate holiness. That's why I've chosen not to get any of the cable-TV sports channels. For me it would be a daily temptation and distraction. It would interfere with my practice of the spiritual disciplines, and I don't want that to happen.

What will it take for you? Disconnecting your cable service? Watching one football game on Sundays rather than two? Throwing the TV set into the nearest dumpster? Skipping television completely for a month? Take whatever action is necessary to make sure you have this habit under control.

PRIME TIME HOLINESS

The television industry calls evenings and weekends, when most people are free to watch their programs, "prime time." The problem is that prime time television viewing conflicts with the prime time for Christians to cultivate the habits of holiness...

Early on I learned that our family did not fit into commercial breaks or after eleven p.m. From our frustration we realized that we could choose either family time or TV time. Together we chose family time and turned the television off.

— David McKenna

I'm learning that people can hate a lot of television, hate their own viewing habits, hate what it does to them and their families, and still think it's bizarre that anybody wants to get rid of it.[1]

— Jerry Mander

The Church would be revolutionized if Christians would reverse the amount of time they spend on two things: watching TV and reading their Bible.

— Derek Prince

2 After studying this chapter, you visit a friend who is glued to a 12-hour extravaganza of *Gilligan's Island* reruns. Removing him/her from the TV set may require amputation. How should you respond?

❏ Make some popcorn and join the fun

❏ Leave in self-righteous disgust

❏ Turn off the TV and begin lecturing from this book

❏ Exercise love instead of judgment

❏ Throw both your friend and the TV into the nearest dumpster

---

Meditate on Ephesians 5:15-17. Do you view time with the sense of urgency Paul describes here?

At best, this week's prime-time attraction will affect you for a week or two. By contrast, if you turn off the TV and spend that same time slot practicing the spiritual disciplines, you will be affected for eternity.

So go ahead—try it. All you'll miss is the latest TV show or movie (most of which are well worth missing anyway). In its place you will be positioning yourself to hear the voice of God and experience intimacy with your Father.

Videos and movies. A few years ago I read a magazine article confirming my worst fears on the subject of videos, movies, and the church:

> While Hollywood films have become an integral part of contemporary society, most Christians would say that they neither go to the movies nor watch television. Yet that assertion is a myth. Actually, most Christian households watch the same movies and the same television programming in the same percentages as non-Christians. The only difference is that Christians add a portion of religious programming to their viewing diet.[3]

Ted Baehr, a Christian film critic quoted in the same article, says, "The overwhelming majority of Christians in

> **❝** Have you ever spent an evening or a Saturday with your eyes glued to the television? You should do a dozen things, but you keep gawking at the inane objects wiggling before you. Afterwards, you sense an empty feeling in your stomach knowing you have spent four or five utterly wasted hours and you will never again have those hours back to use.[2] **❞**
>
> **— Jerry White**

the U.S. have the same media habits as the non-Christian population."

Do you hear that? Not a handful of particularly weak believers, but *the overwhelming majority.* If this is accurate, it's unacceptable.

It doesn't surprise me that bored, directionless unbelievers constantly distract themselves with movies. But why is it that Christians are sitting bug-eyed in front of the big screen just as often?

---

3 Would you be willing to have all the movies you have seen in the past six months printed in next week's church bulletin? Why or why not?

Obviously, some movies are worth seeing. (Most of these, unfortunately, were done before 1950, so get used to enjoying black and white.) But if we were honestly to evaluate the majority of today's films it would be two thumbs down. They simply lack redemptive qualities. They don't contribute to our pursuit of godliness. In fact, they desensitize us to sin and subtly erode our desire to pursue God.

Meditate on 1 Corinthians 10:23. Too many Christians get hung up on a system of do's and don'ts. What litmus test does Paul recommend for evaluating our activities?

I have no desire to be the Church's equivalent of Siskel and/or Ebert. Instead, let me encourage you to develop biblical criteria for evaluating movies. Here are two verses that will help you gain discernment regarding entertainment: "So whether you eat or drink or whatever you do, do it all for the glory of God" (1Co 10:31). "[G]ive thanks in all circumstances, for this is God's will for you in Christ Jesus" (1Th 5:18).

Allow these biblical principles to sharpen your discernment and determine your viewing priorities. If you can't watch a particular movie to the glory of God, don't. If you can't give God thanks for the TV show you're watching, stop watching it.

Hobbies and sports. The biblically informed Christian recognizes that time for leisure is a gift from God. But that's far different from "working for the weekend." In a culture that curses Mondays and worships Fridays, we should continually assess whether our leisure time has taken on too high a priority.

---

4 Check the advertising slogan you think best reflects America's attitude toward leisure:

❏ "For those with time for quality" (Benson & Hedges cigarettes)

❏ "It just doesn't get any better than this" (Old Milwaukee beer)

❏ "Only your time is more precious than this watch" (Omega watches)

❏ "We build excitement" (Pontiac automobiles)

❏ "You deserve a break today" (McDonald's restaurants)

❏ "Fortunately, every day comes with an evening" (Windsor Canadian whiskey)

I have no doubt God takes pleasure when a woman decorates her home, or a father attends a football game with his son. Yet as I listen to people rave on about their favorite hobby or a particular sports team, I sometimes discover a corresponding lack of passion for Jesus and the church. These enthusiasts apparently invest lots of time into this area of interest, but they just can't seem to find time for the spiritual disciplines or regular participation in their local church.

> ❝ One of the significant measures of a person's spiritual commitment is what he does with his discretionary or leisure time.[4] ❞
>
> — **Jerry White**

We are commanded to "find out what pleases the Lord," (Ep 5:10) and do it. Can you imagine that God is pleased when our love for sports or hobbies is stronger than our love for him?

Careers. With increasing intensity, corporate America is demanding excessive allegiance from its work force. Men and women are expected to sacrifice anything—time, family, integrity—in exchange for upward mobility. As you can

For Further Study:
If you'd like a biblical view on the importance of work, read 2Th 3:6-13; Ac 18:3, 20:34-35; 1Co 4:12; and 1Th 2:9.

imagine, devotion to the Lord and his Church aren't considered as valid priorities, if they are considered at all.

This is not to encourage laziness or irresponsibility, nor am I bashing anyone who seeks to honor God through diligent service on the job. Work is a gift from God and a significant part of his call on our lives. He uses our work as a way to meet financial needs, develop our character, and advance the gospel.

My concern is for those who have allowed career to eclipse their passion for Jesus Christ and his kingdom. Over time, they have lost their radical edge. They are no longer hearing God's voice consistently. They substitute "quality time" with their families for "quantity time." They attend church, but their hearts are at the office.

 How many hours, on average, do you spend each week on the job? (Homemakers included)

- ☐ 30-40 hours
- ☐ 40-50 hours
- ☐ 50-60 hours
- ☐ 60-80 hours
- ☐ More than 80 hours

I'm privileged to serve a church filled with people who have as their passion and priority God and his purpose, not their careers. There's Joann, who graduated from M.I.T. with a degree in architecture. Rather than making big money at a prestigious firm, she has chosen to work free-lance in order to care for people in the church. Ed could be retired and fishing his life away in Florida. Instead, he serves others through his involvement with the church's marriage-counseling team, and oversees the teaching-tape

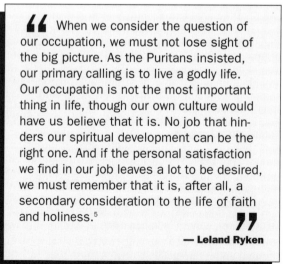

❝ When we consider the question of our occupation, we must not lose sight of the big picture. As the Puritans insisted, our primary calling is to live a godly life. Our occupation is not the most important thing in life, though our own culture would have us believe that it is. No job that hinders our spiritual development can be the right one. And if the personal satisfaction we find in our job leaves a lot to be desired, we must remember that it is, after all, a secondary consideration to the life of faith and holiness.[5] **❞**

— Leland Ryken

Meditate on Acts 2:37-41. In response to Peter's sermon on the day of Pentecost, about 3,000 people—including many foreigners who were just visiting Jerusalem for Passover—were added to the church. Imagine how many of them sacrificed careers at home in order to participate in God's purpose.

ministry. Larry travels the country for the federal government, but makes a point of adjusting his schedule so that his leadership of a small group and attendance at Sunday meetings are not needlessly interrupted. Many in our church have turned down promotions because they involved relocation.

People like this aren't interested in attracting attention to themselves. They just want to serve, and they haven't allowed the culture to seduce them. While pursuing excellence in their work, they haven't let that work distract them from their primary priority and passion—Jesus Christ and his advancing kingdom. Their selfless example provokes me on a daily basis.

---

6 Congratulations! You've been offered a significant promotion. It comes with a huge salary increase, and puts you in line for an even better job in just a few more years. This is it ... the big time awaits!

There's just one little catch. To take the job you will have to relocate to another city 1,500 miles away.

How would you rank the following factors in terms of their importance in shaping your decision?

(1=highest priority, 6=lowest priority. Give each factor a different ranking)

_____ Salary and benefits

_____ Price of real estate

_____ Career advancement

_____ Church

_____ Climate/geography

_____ Proximity to family/friends

This kind of radical obedience should be the norm. God is establishing churches that are full of people fully prepared to climb off the career ladder—should God direct them to—because they want to build something that is far more meaningful and significant. These men and women won't allow themselves to be jerked around by corporate transfers, compiling possessions and positions at the expense of their relationships with God, their family, and their church. Nor will they have any regrets when God one day summarizes their lives with a resounding, "Well done!"

Initial Sacrifice, Eternal Reward

Has anything diminished your appetite—your passion—for God? It could be something minor, something that appears insignificant. A fascination with news, for example. An opportunity for promotion. An intriguing hobby. A dream vacation. Something so seemingly justifiable that you haven't even thought of reevaluating it.

> ❝ God has given us the Spiritual Disciplines as a means of receiving His grace and growing in godliness.... We have learned that the Spiritual Disciplines are scriptural paths where we may expect to encounter the transforming grace of God.[6] ❞
>
> **— Donald Whitney**

But here's the issue: Is it competing with God as your primary passion? Once you recognize that something—anything—is hindering your growth in godliness, please don't waste any time in attacking and avoiding it.

As we remove these hindrances, let's replace them with the spiritual disciplines of prayer, meditation, Bible study, fasting, confession, and solitude. What may initially seem like a sacrifice won't compare to the reward of intimacy with the One who made us for himself. ■

GROUP DISCUSSION

1. We've all seen images of starving children. What signs would indicate that a Christian is starving spiritually?

2. Discuss how seemingly innocent activities can become idols in our lives.

3. How can we respond to conviction without getting trapped by guilt?

4. Is it possible to be spiritually hungry without *feeling* ravenous for God?

5. How do you react to Jerry Mander's quote about television on page 92?

6. Suppose you were offered a job transfer with a 20% salary increase. What steps would you take in making a decision?

7. What is the difference between rest and leisure?

8. If you were to list your dreams on one side of a sheet of

paper and God's purposes on the other side, how would they compare?

9. Do you sense a need to increase your appetite for God? What first step can you take?

RECOMMENDED READING

Desiring God by John Piper (Sisters, OR: Multnomah Books, 1986)

A Call to Spiritual Reformation by D.A. Carson (Grand Rapids, MI: Baker Book House, 1992)

Religious Affections by Jonathan Edwards (Minneapolis, MN: Bethany Book Publishers, 1996)

Answer to Warm-Up
(from page 89): *Jurassic Park* (E) is the most profitable, having grossed $976.1 million in ticket sales worldwide. Combined revenue from these six films adds up to $4.4 billion. That could have financed the printing of approximately 2.5 billion Bibles for distribution in Asia and Eastern Europe.

NOTES   **STUDY ONE** – Only One Thing Is Needed

1. Charles E. Hummel, *Tyranny of the Urgent* (Downers Grove, IL: InterVarsity Press, 1967).
2. 2 John 10:14, 27
3. Charles E. Hummel, *Tyranny of the Urgent*

STUDY TWO – Train Yourself to Be Godly

1. Dallas Willard, *The Spirit of the Disciplines* (San Francisco, CA: HarperCollins Publishers, 1991), pp.3-4.
2. Jerry Bridges, *The Practice of Godliness* (Colorado Springs, CO: NavPress, 1983), p.75-76.
3. Sinclair B. Ferguson, *Grow in Grace* (Carlisle, PA: The Banner of Truth Trust, 1989), p.20.
4. Dallas Willard, *The Spirit of the Disciplines*, p.6.
5. Jerry White, *The Power of Commitment* (Colorado Springs, CO: NavPress, 1985), p.131.

STUDY THREE – Prayer: Direct Dial to Heaven

1. Donald Whitney, *Spiritual Disciplines for the Christian Life* (Colorado Springs, CO: NavPress, 1991), p.65.
2. E.M. Bounds, *Power Through Prayer* (Grand Rapids, MI: Zondervan Publishing House), p.12.
3. Quoted in *Martin Luther's Quiet Time* by Walter Trobisch (Downer's Grove, IL: InterVarsity Press, 1975).
4. Charles E. Hummel, *Tyranny of the Urgent* (Downers Grove, IL: InterVarsity Press, 1967).
5. E.M. Bounds, *Power Through Prayer*, p.26.
6. Oswald Chambers, *My Utmost for His Highest* (New York: Dodd, Mead and Company, 1935), p.236.

STUDY FOUR – Meditation: Not Just for Gurus

1. The author's expanded paraphrase.
2. Donald Whitney, *Spiritual Disciplines for the Christian Life* (Colorado Springs, CO: NavPress, 1991), p.45.
3. Henry Scougal, *The Life of God in the Soul of Man* (Harrisonburg, VA: Sprinkle Publications).
4. Quoted in Donald Whitney, *Spiritual Disciplines for the Christian Life*, p.187.
5. Jerry Bridges, *The Practice of Godliness* (Colorado Springs, CO: NavPress, 1983), p.43.
6. A.W. Tozer, *The Pursuit of God* (Camp Hill, PA: Christian Publications, Inc., 1982), p.75.
7. Bruce Olson as told to Susan DeVore Williams, "Bruce Olson's Nine-Month Colombian Captivity" (*Charisma and Christian Life*, November 1989).
8. A.W. Tozer, *The Pursuit of God*, p.82.
9. R.C. Sproul, *Knowing Scripture* (Downers Grove, IL: InterVarsity Press, 1977).
10. John Piper, *Desiring God: Meditations of a Christian Hedonist* (Sisters, OR: Multnomah Books, 1996), p.128.
11. Barna Research Group, *The Church Today: Insightful Statistics and Commentary* (Glendale, CA, 1990).

STUDY FIVE – Fasting: When Hunger = Power

1. Arthur Wallis, *God's Chosen Fast* (Fort Washington, PA: Christian Literature Crusade, 1968), p.45.

2. Richard Foster, *Celebration of Discipline* (San Francisco, CA: Harper & Row, 1988), pp.47-48.
3. Andrew Murray, *With Christ in the School of Prayer* (Westwood, NJ: Fleming H. Revell Co., 1965).
4. Arthur Wallis, *God's Chosen Fast*, p.50.
5. Ibid., p.56.
6. Thomas À Kempis, Irwin Edman, ed., *The Consolations of Philosophy* (New York: Random House, Modern Library, 1943), p.152.
7. Donald Whitney, "Fasting: The Misunderstood Discipline" (*Discipleship Journal*, Issue 67).

STUDY SIX – Confession: Doorway to Life
1. Dallas Willard, *The Spirit of the Disciplines*, (San Francisco, CA: HarperCollins Publishers, 1988), p.188.
2. Roland Bainton, *Here I Stand: A Life of Martin Luther* (Nashville, TN: Abingdon, 1950), p.225.
3. Richard Foster, *Celebration of Discipline* (San Francisco, CA: Harper & Row, 1988), p.157.
4. Quoted in *Celebration of Discipline* by Richard Foster, p.143.
5. Dietrich Bonhoeffer, *Life Together* (San Francisco, CA: Harper & Row, 1954), p.116.
6. Ken Sande, *The Peacemaker* (Grand Rapids, MI; Baker Book House, 1991), pp.94-102.

STUDY SEVEN – Solitude: Getting Alone with God
1. Donald Whitney, *Spiritual Disciplines for the Christian Life* (Colorado Springs, CO: NavPress, 1991), p.185.
2. A.W. Tozer, *The Pursuit of God* (Camp Hill, PA: Christian Publications, Inc., 1982), p.80.
3. Dallas Willard, *The Spirit of the Disciplines* (San Francisco, CA: HarperCollins Publishers, 1991), p.160.
4. Louis Bouyer, *The Spirituality of the New Testament and the Fathers, vol. 1 of A History of Christian Spirituality* (New York: Seabury, 1982), p.313.
5. Quoted in Donald Whitney, *Spiritual Disciplines for the Christian Life*, p.193.
6. Dietrich Bonhoeffer, *Life Together* (San Francisco, CA: Harper & Row, 1954), p.77.
7. Nancy Gibbs, "How America Has Run Out of Time" (*Time* magazine, April 24, 1989).
8. Ibid.
9. Henry Scougal, *The Life of God in the Soul of Man* (Harrisonburg, VA: Sprinkle Publications), p.107.

STUDY EIGHT – An Appetite for God
1. Jerry Mander, *Four Arguments For The Elimination of Television* (New York: Wm. Morrow & Co., 1978).
2. Jerry White, *The Power of Commitment* (Colorado Springs, CO: NavPress, 1985), p.67.
3. Mike Yorkey, *Citizen* magazine, January, 1989
4. Jerry White, *The Power of Commitment*, p.68.
5. Leland Ryken, *Work and Leisure in Christian Perspective* (Portland, OR: Multnomah Press, 1987), p.151.
6. Donald Whitney, *Spiritual Disciplines for the Christian Life* (Colorado Springs, CO: NavPress, 1991) pp.16 & 28.

OTHER TITLES IN PDI'S *PURSUIT OF GODLINESS* SERIES

THIS GREAT SALVATION   **Robin Boisvert and C.J. Mahaney**

Countless Christians struggle through life feeling condemned and confused. No matter how much they do for God, they never feel quite sure of his acceptance.

Sound at all familiar? Then you'll find *great* news in *This Great Salvation*. Start enjoying a new measure of grace and peace at every level of your Christian life as this unique book reveals anew what God has done for you through Christ. (112 pages)

HOW CAN I CHANGE?   **Robin Boisvert and C.J. Mahaney**

How Can I Change? (originally titled *From Glory to Glory*) rests on a remarkable assumption: If you will study and apply the doctrine of sanctification, any sin can be overcome.

Have you known the frustration of falling short in your efforts to please God? Have you questioned whether you will *ever* be able to change? If so, this book will have a profound impact on your walk with Christ. (112 pages)

LOVE THAT LASTS   **Gary and Betsy Ricucci**

A magnificent marriage is more than wishful thinking. It can and should be the experience of every husband and wife willing to follow God's plan for them as a couple.

Whether your marriage is new, needy, or simply ready for a refresher, here is an excellent guide for helping you build a thriving, lasting love. (176 pages)

WALKING WITH THE WISE   **Benny and Sheree Phillips**

At last...a book to keep your hopes and standards high during the adolescent years! Written for parents and teens to use together, *Walking With The Wise* hits the "big issues" such as dating, peer pressure, and passion for God.

Reinforce your relationship...and strengthen your convictions...with this one-of-a-kind resource for parents and teens. (192 pages)

FIRST STEPS OF FAITH   **Steve Shank**

Other than a Bible, what's the first resource you would give a brand-new Christian? *First Steps of Faith* will meet that critical need.

Using vivid, personal illustrations, Steve Shank lays a solid yet simple foundation for a lifetime of growth. Mature Christians will also find plenty of meat as they explore the attributes of God, our battle against indwelling sin, and much more. (112 pages)

WHY SMALL GROUPS?   **C.J. Mahaney, General Editor**

Not simply a how-to guide, this illuminating book starts by answering the all-important question of *why* a church needs small groups. The short answer? Because small groups are invaluable in helping us to "work out our salvation together" in practical, biblical ways.

Specially developed for leaders and members of small groups alike, *Why Small Groups?* is loaded with insight, wisdom, and practical instruction. This book can put you on the fast track to Christian maturity. (144 pages)

ADDITIONAL RESOURCES FROM PDI COMMUNICATIONS

PRAISE AND WORSHIP MUSIC

PDI worship songs have been in use for more than a decade in local churches around the world. By the grace and mercy of God, more than 10,000 churches in the United States alone currently use these Christ-centered, Cross-centered songs to worship and glorify God. PDI Music's *Come and Worship* series features four releases per year, two of them documenting live worship experiences.

"I consider the music of PDI to be a powerful resource for what God is doing in praise and worship today."
worship leader Kent Henry

"If I could only have one source for new songs, I'd choose PDI."
Tom Kraeuter, former Managing Editor, *Psalmist Magazine*

"I can think of no single greater resource to the body of Christ at large than the music and teaching resources of PDI."
David Estes, Director of A&R, Word Music

TEACHING TAPES

Powerful messages on growth in holiness, raising teens, biblical masculinity, leadership issues, and much more.

SOVEREIGN GRACE MAGAZINE

In circulation for more than 15 years, this bimonthly publication addresses the most critical issues facing Christians today. It also profiles the people and progress of PDI's team-related churches in the United States and abroad.

For a catalog of PDI resources and a free issue of *Sovereign Grace*, call **1-800-736-2202** or write to us:

PDI Communications
7881 Beechcraft Avenue, Suite B
Gaithersburg, MD 20879
Attention: Resource Center

email:pdi@pdinet.org
fax: 301-948-7833

Please visit our Web site at www.pdinet.org